Martial Arts
of the Orient

Martial Arts
of the Orient

general editor: Bryn Williams
special photography: Bob Hope

Hamlyn
London · New York · Sydney · Toronto

Published by
The Hamlyn Publishing Group Limited
London · New York · Sydney · Toronto
Astronaut House, Feltham, Middlesex, England

© Copyright The Hamlyn Publishing Group Limited 1975
Reprinted 1976
ISBN 0 600 35229 3

Printed in England by
Jarrold and Sons Limited, Norwich

Contents

Introduction

Unlike Europe which emerged from feudalism in the fifteenth century, Japan became a modern state only in the second half of the nineteenth century. Until its forced opening to Western trade in 1853–4 and the succession to the throne of the young modernizing Emperor Meiji in 1867, Japan was a feudal society policed by samurai. It is largely from the fighting skills of the samurai that the martial arts described in this book are derived.

Although the Japanese are a proud and insular people, their culture shows evidence of extensive borrowings from mainland China. This borrowing has affected the spheres of art, architecture, poetry, Confucianism, and the written script as well as Zen Buddhism, military strategy, and individual fighting techniques. The latter three aspects are particularly relevant to the subject matter of this book. Only two of the fighting arts covered (kung fu and tai chi) are uniquely and solely Chinese. Some are Okinawan, but most are Japanese. However, the book has been called *Martial Arts of the Orient*, rather than *Martial Arts of Japan*, not only because of the apparent origins of the arts but because the cultural interplay between Japan and China has been such that it is very difficult to isolate one from the other.

Feudal Japan was a class-based society with the divinely appointed emperor at the apex. However, by the eighth century AD actual power had begun to move into the hands of a series of military and administrative dictators known as *shoguns*, and the emperors were withdrawing from politics into the conscious patronage of art and culture. Late in the twelfth century this process was complete, and the great Shogun Yoritomo proceeded to unify Japan and impose a rigidly hierarchical society in which the emperor was supported, in descending order of social significance, by the shogun, the *daimyo* or great nobles, the *bushi* or military knights, the food-producing peasants, the artisans, and the merchants.

The maintenance of any hierarchical society requires the backing of force, hence the emergence of the bushi or samurai as they came to be known in the West. In fact 'samurai' originally meant 'servant' and they were therefore the lower members of the bushi class. These samurai, who owed their allegiance to individual daimyo, were posted in every district and served primarily as policemen and tax collectors. They had substantial privileges, were exempt taxes, and had the legal right to kill a disrespectful commoner on the spot. To prevent them from exploiting their position, a samurai code of ethics known as *bushido* (literally meaning 'military knight ways', that is the code of conduct proper to a fighting knight) came into being. In many respects it was similar to the Western codes of knightly chivalry of approximately the same period and stressed bravery, honour, truthfulness, politeness, and the capacity for self-control and self-sacrifice. Doubtless there were occasions when both codes were observed more in theory than practice.

The symbol of the samurai was the sword and even today kendo is accepted as being the senior and most traditional *budo* (fighting way) discipline. This veneration of the sword dates back to the mythological origin of Japan. Legend has it that the god and goddess Izanhei and Izanami gave birth to Japan and appointed the sun goddess Amaterasu to rule over the heavens. It was the grandson of Amaterasu who, equipped with the imperial treasures of sword, mirror, and necklace, descended from the heavens to rule Japan, and it was his great-grandson, Jimmu-Tenno, who became the first human emperor in 1660 BC. From these mythological origins stem the belief by all Japanese until recent times in the divine ancestry of their emperors, the veneration of the sword as part of the imperial regalia of the royal family, the existence of Japan's most widespread religion Shinto, 'the way of the gods', and the symbol of the rising sun in the national flag.

The skills of the samurai consisted primarily of swordsmanship, archery, the use of the spear, horsemanship, ju-jutsu, which the warrior used in close-contact situations when deprived of weapons, and the appreciation of tactics. As time passed, changes in weapons and their usage naturally occurred as the result of innovation. For example, when the original long and heavy *naginata*, or straight-bladed spear, was found to be ineffectual in combat, it was, in a lighter form, relegated to a woman's weapon for use in the defence of the home. Similarly battle archery eventually declined when it

Budo training in a variety of forms from a nineteenth-century print. Illustrated amongst other arts are ba-jutsu, jutte-jutsu, ho-jutsu, iai-jutsu, so-jutsu, naginata-jutsu, kendo, kenjutsu, kusarigama-jutsu, bo-jutsu, ju-jutsu, and kyudo. A veritable *tour de force*. Roald Knutsen collection.

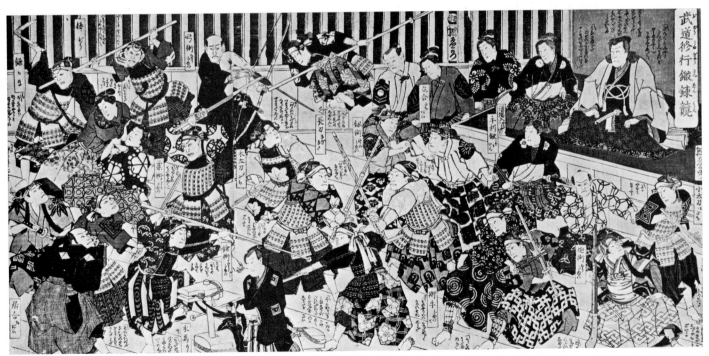

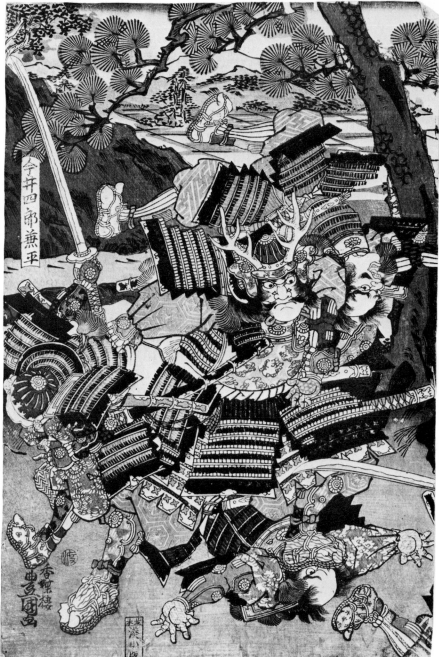

right A typical battlefield mêlée. Note the totemic head-dress and the loose-flowing hair— both designed to frighten hapless opponents. Print by Toyokuni II. Victoria and Albert Museum, London.

Modern followers of kyudo (*above*) and kendo (*below right*). In ceremonial archery and kendo-kata, the immediacy of the old *jutsu* or battle techniques have been left far behind.

was appreciated that battles fought from great distances and from behind covered positions were not decisive. With the development of matchlocks in the sixteenth century, the archer became an even less significant part of the daimyo's army. *Kyujutsu* (battlefield archery) fell into disuse and *kyudo* (the way of the archer) developed as a non-lethal alternative with the emphasis upon personal spiritual development.

A further example of this evolution can be seen in the transformation of *kenjutsu* (fighting with the sword) into *kendo* (the way of the sword), which was ultimately to be practised with bamboo swords and protective clothing. This process began during the politically stable Tokugawa period when the need and opportunity for practical application of fighting skills diminished. It became even more pronounced during the Meiji period after the samurai had been disestablished and the opportunities for realistic combat ceased altogether. The fact that kyudo and kendo both end in *do*, pronounced dō as in 'stow' and meaning 'the way' or more fully 'the way to enlightenment, self-realization, and understanding', is significant. It indicates that they have been transformed from a practical means of combat to an educational form with the emphasis on the personal development of the participant. This Zen element is reflected to various degrees in aikido, judo, karate-do, naginata-do, iai-do, etc.

It was during the Kamakura period that Zen came into prominence in Japan and achieved there its fullest flowering. Like popular Buddhism it denies the power of the intellect, extols that of intuition, and aims at enlightenment through freedom from illusion and passion. Individuality it considers to be an illusion, and its ultimate aim is identification with, or submergence in, the world and the universe. However, unlike Buddhism in general, Zen advocates action, discipline, and self-cultivation. It is action not words. Attracted by its concepts of loyalty, indifference to physical hardships, total commitment, stoical trust in fate, and disdain for

The great twelfth-century inter-clan struggles of the Minamoto and Taira were a prelude to the establishment of a rigidly hierarchical society in Japan. Print by Yoshikazu. Victoria and Albert Museum, London.

life, Zen naturally appealed to the warrior classes and became virtually their religion, although it cannot properly be called a religion. It is more a way of life. *Yari-jutsu*, or the use of the straight-bladed spear, and ju-jutsu are the only indigenous Japanese martial arts not to acquire this do form.

Although different *ryu* or schools of ju-jutsu existed, this form of hand-to-hand fighting was designed to be a comprehensive type of unarmed combat, involving a whole range of punching, kicking, gouging, throwing, locking, strangulation, and groundwork techniques. With the ending of feudalism many of the ryu, which had been supported by the daimyo, were disbanded. To a modern society ju-jutsu as a whole and certainly its practical application was unacceptable. To be tolerated, practitioners had to utilize only certain elements of the art and develop the activity along narrower and more acceptable lines.

Dr Kano, for example, removed many of the more dangerous techniques, and by organizing the throwing, locking, strangulation, and groundwork on a scientific basis he developed judo. Many of the more dangerous locks—to the fingers, wrist, knee, and foot— were forbidden and only those to the elbow and shoulder were retained. Such developments enabled judo to become acceptable in schools, and eventually to gain the status of a modern Olympic sport. Meanwhile, Morei Uyeshiba was developing aikido, with its emphasis upon wrist throws, restraining locks, and utilization of the opponent's movements, and its avoidance of the close-grappling situations used in judo. To some extent therefore ju-jutsu was being broken down into its constituent elements, and great emphasis was placed not only on the sporting aspect but more particularly upon its character-building qualities.

In the very early Meiji period the government actively discouraged the practice of the fighting arts and it was only a romantic feeling towards tradition that kept them alive. Eventually, however, in an attempt to develop within the general populace the sense of discipline and morality formerly possessed by the samurai, the government came to accept them as part of the educational programme. The emphasis upon practical combat was inevitably less significant and the do or training element became increasingly important. In other words the government was using traditional methods for a political, nationalistic, and educational objective rather as rugby football was developed in the British public schools to cultivate team-spirit and courage. In 1890 the Japanese Minister of Education, himself an ex-samurai, incorporated sumo, kendo, and judo into the school programme for boys and naginata-do for girls. In 1911 kendo and judo became compulsory in all middle schools.

Then, in the early twentieth century, into this very nationalistic and educationally orientated scene came a foreign influence: karate. Arriving from Okinawa in 1917 at the invitation of the Ministry of Education, Funakoshi Gichin gave a series of demonstrations, primarily to intellectual audiences. Although a great exponent of tang or Chinese hand, as karate was then called, Funakoshi, a teacher by profession, was selected as much for his lecturing as his technical ability. His demonstrations were highly successful and in 1923 he returned to teach permanently in Japan

opposite Bhodhidharma, the bringer of Zen meditation to China (*below left*), seen through the eyes of a late nineteenth-century artist, and two views of modern Zen in Japan: a garden of contemplation at the Ryoanji temple in Kyoto (*above*) and the reading of scriptures at the Enkakuji temple (*below right*).

top Utsuri-goshi, an advanced judo technique that involves switching the opponent from one hip to the other, mid-throw.

above Kote-gaeshi, an aikido throw in which the defender's outward tension on the attacker's wrist has resulted in the attacker throwing himself over his own arm.

top A karate *Taisho*: a powerful attacking blow to the jaw follows up a practical deflecting block with the left hand.

above A group of kendoka sitting *mokuzo* to compose the mind before and after training.

and was followed there by several other Okinawan instructors.

However, Okinawan fighting techniques had never been greatly influenced by Zen nor did they possess a do element. They were fundamentally utilitarian and lacked the more academic or intellectual aspect of the samurai-based skills. Tang hand upon its arrival in Japan was therefore foreign in more ways than one. However, the Japanese are, when they wish to be, great assimilators of foreign ideas, and they were readily able to absorb the new skills, grafting on to them an indigenous do element until in 1936 they dropped the name 'tang hand' and substituted 'karate-do', meaning 'the way of the empty-hand'. Karate had indeed become Japanese.

Common factors in the martial arts

One feature common to all the martial arts is the state of *zanshin* or total awareness which practitioners endeavour to cultivate. This is not a state that is achieved through an intellectual analysis of environment but rather one that, through experience, evolves naturally and instinctively. By an intense and intuitive use of the senses some exponents seem to achieve a state of awareness that almost suggests sixth sense. This is the awareness of, and involvement in, environment for which Zen practitioners aim. It produces an intriguing calmness of mind and an apparent detachment even in threatening situations when fear or anger might seem the natural reaction. An expert reacts not in a personalized way but almost like an applied natural law—the lightning strikes so the thunder sounds, the wind blows so the tree bends, the attack comes, the response is automatic.

Another feature of all the martial arts is the element of spirit and commitment, which is largely explained by their common samurai origin and which was subsequently positively encouraged by the

Meiji educational system. For the samurai, fighting was a serious business – a matter of life or death, not a game to be won or lost. Commitment was therefore fundamentally important. Despite the obvious reduction in basic danger and fundamental seriousness, this quality has been largely retained in all the martial arts. That this is so is possibly one of the reasons why the martial arts can still claim to have some character-building qualities.

All martial arts are practised in a hall known as a *dojo*, which translated means 'way place'. The detailed layout depends upon the particular martial art but generally it includes a large wooden floor area, which in the case of judo and aikido will be covered by matting. At the end or sides there may well be training equipment specially devised for the activity concerned, i.e. punching boards for karate. Because of their basic similarity, many dojos can be used for practising a number of martial arts and some clubs have specialized sections in several of the branches.

Clothing is again dependent on the activity but aikido, judo, and karate all use similar lightweight, white suits or *gi*. Because of the pulling and tugging involved, judogi are normally made of stronger, thicker texture than those worn for aikido and karate-do. All three disciplines also use a system of coloured belts to indicate the grade of the wearer. The number of *kyu* or student grades and the colour of the belts used to denote them tend to vary not only with the discipline but also with the particular style within that discipline. The senior or instructor grades are known as *dan* grades and all normally wear black belts.

The atmosphere within a dojo is usually extremely formal and the discipline very strict. The deference with which senior instructors are treated reflects the Japanese hierarchical attitude. In Westernized clubs this attitude is declining somewhat, although the informal trend is more apparent in activities, such as judo, which have a relatively long Western background. The young arts, such as karate, still tend to be very formal. Chinese arts, such as kung fu, also tend to be less formal than their Japanese counterparts. This is partly because the Chinese are in many ways much more informal than the Japanese. They, like Westerners, tend to treat kung fu with less of the formalized do approach and more as a pure means of self-defence or combat. There are naturally exceptions, but as a generalization this is true.

To the onlooker some of the activities that take place inside a dojo are also highly formalized. Kyudo particularly would appear to be 100% formality, with the emphasis entirely upon the manner in which the technique is performed rather than the apparent objective, i.e. the hitting of the target. In the more physically robust activities such as judo or karate the formality in performance is much less apparent, but in the preliminaries to competition it is still very obvious. All the Japanese martial arts retain the use of Japanese terminology. Naturally this adds somewhat to the atmosphere of formality but it also serves as an international language in those activities in which competition applies.

The use of *kata*, or formalized training sequences incorporating a whole range of techniques, is a common denominator of Japanese-based arts. Tai chi, which is Chinese, consists entirely of kata, but

top Total commitment as Billy Higgins of Great Britain, runner-up in the 1972 World Individual Championships, follows a karate Leg Sweep with a downward punch.

above The formal bow. Each time a kendoka enters the dojo he or she makes this sign of respect.

13

Chicago parking-meter maids getting some necessary instruction in judo techniques before they take to the streets.

then it is more a form of exercise than of combat. Kung fu has much less kata influence. However, despite its recent popularity on television and film screens, relatively little is known about kung fu. Only slowly are the genuine kung-fu experts beginning to emerge in the West. Because of the much greater readiness of Japan to export its martial knowledge, considerably more is known about the arts originating in those islands.

A final common factor is the emphasis upon breathing and stomach strengthening. Breathing is of the diaphragmatic kind, with the air being drawn into the lower lungs by strong use of the stomach muscles rather than shallowly into the upper lungs as is more normal. This type of breathing can greatly assist muscular tension and it also encourages solidity of stance and explosiveness of action. Explosive movement in all the martial arts is in fact always accompanied by a *kiai* or yell, which comes more from the stomach than the throat. This yell co-ordinates naturally with the breathing, assists muscle contraction, boosts explosiveness, provides a psychological focus for the movement, and may momentarily shatter the opponent's concentration, thus leaving open a line of attack.

Although the differences between, let us say, kyudo and karate are apparently very considerable, there are, as has been shown, several common threads—historical, philosophical, and psychological as well as technical—that link all the martial arts.

Self-defence and violence

The attraction of the martial arts both in general and in particular varies from individual to individual. However, there is certainly a large number of people attracted by its self-defence potential. At one time judo was the main focus of interest, but, since it became an Olympic sport, it has tended to play down this image and stress the sport approach. Karate, kung fu, and ju-jutsu, however, most certainly attract those who feel themselves to be in need of an instant personal deterrent and wish to be stronger, fitter, and more self-confident in what is a progressively more violent age. This urge has undoubtedly been accentuated by the recent flood of James Bond, kung fu, karate, and Hong Kong originated films, many of which exploit the theme of violence behind a thin veneer of idealism. When a popular film is released, the effect upon applications for karate and kung-fu clubs is almost instantaneous and sometimes overwhelming. Such a situation naturally contains social dangers. To assume that all those initially attracted by these films are by nature self-disciplined is obviously unrealistic.

A good club, however, can overcome this problem because both the external discipline and the self-discipline required is such that individuals with no capacity for either quickly fall by the wayside. Those who stay will certainly become potentially more dangerous combatants but the chances of them using their skill in undisciplined out-of-dojo situations are substantially reduced. This statement applies, of course, to a good club. It does not apply to a bad one, where an instructor with an undesirable attitude can have the most frightful effect upon his students. This dilemma is enlarged upon in the karate section, and it is the writer's contention that serious

Karate students practising *kiai* tune themselves up to a high 'attacking' frame of mind.

Much of the martial arts' recent press has been bad, with reporters playing up the connection between karate or kung fu and violence.

thought should be given to the official licensing of instructors by recognizing those of responsible national organizations and that without approved qualifications instructors should not be permitted to advertise or teach.

If the best of what the fighting arts have to offer can be retained, strong and responsible administration developed, and the incursions of exploiters curbed, the West will learn to be pleasantly surprised by what the martial arts have to offer. If not, we may live to regret, at least in this limited sphere, the accuracy of Napoleon's forecast:

Let China sleep—when she awakes the world will tremble.

Weaponry

Kendo
Roald Knutsen

Iai-jutsu and iai-do
Roald Knutsen

Kyudo
John Piper

Naginata-do
Roald Knutsen

Yari-jutsu
Roald Knutsen

Okinawan weaponry
Roald Knutsen

Kendo

Kendo is the art of Japanese swordsmanship. It is immediately identifiable in everyone's mind with the Japanese sword and the samurai or warrior class of Old Japan. The sword was the soul of the samurai, and the history of the sword is very much the history of Japan. But when we talk of kendo we have to recognize three quite distinct forms. The earliest is kenjutsu or the techniques used before about 1590; the second is kendo, in which swordsmanship assumed an intellectual and philosophical character; and lastly there is modern kendo, which is at least partly sport-orientated.

The first known reference to swordsmanship can be traced back as far as the year AD 789, when *kumitachi* (sword exercise) was introduced as instruction for the sons of the *kuge*, or noblemen, at the then capital city of Nara. But the roots must surely go back to classical Chinese times more than two thousand years ago. The introduction of kumitachi is still commemorated in the Boys' Festival held each year on 5 May and marked annually by a huge kendo meeting at Kyoto. Although the Nara and Heian periods were eras of great cultural advance, those parts of Japan not in direct contact with the capital were continually plagued by uprisings, banditry, or raiding by the indigenous inhabitants, the Emishi. It was the hardship of provincial life and the necessity for the noble absentee landlords to protect their interests that quickly led to the emergence of a warrior strata in society, the *bushi*. Perhaps it is worthwhile noting that the term 'samurai' originally meant 'a servant'. The more correct term for a warrior is 'bushi', hence *budo* and *bushido* (the warrior's way). In the year 1189 the bushi of the Minamoto clan finally gained complete control of effective government and this they maintained without a break right down to 1868.

There are no records of systematic methods of swordsmanship before the middle of the fourteenth century but ample evidence exists that many warriors in the early period had great skill at arms. The doyen of all Japanese boys, the famous warrior-monk Saito Musashi-bo Benkei (died *circa* 1190) who vowed to take a thousand swords by force of arms in single combat, is one example. It is said that Benkei was defeated at the very last sword by the youthful Minamoto Yoshitsune and thus became Yoshitsune's chief retainer. Certainly throughout kendo history many efforts were made by swordsmen to give more credence to the special *ryu*, or schools, by producing a written genealogy tracing their line back to Yoshitsune!

In Europe, in Carolingian, Saxon, and Viking times famous swords were thought to possess magical properties that transmitted to their owners great advantages in battle. Similar beliefs existed in Japan but with the important difference that in Japan the sword was already one of the three imperial symbols, divinely bestowed and therefore clearly associated with the godhead. By the fourteenth and fifteenth centuries the founders of regular schools of swordsmanship nearly always claimed their inspiration after a final period of prayer, practice, and purification at a Shinto shrine.

Tradition has it that Minamoto Yoshitsune was taught the use of the sword by the mythological race of *tengu*, a cross between goblins and birds, who lived on Mount Heizan near Kyoto. I have in my possession a *tora-no-maki* or record scroll of a minor kendo school that flourished in the eighteenth and early nineteenth centuries and it depicts some forms of kenjutsu being performed by tengu. If the gods did not invent kendo, then lesser beings certainly did. Incidentally, this tora-no-maki claims Yoshitsune as the originator of the school.

According to kendo historians, the earliest school of swordsmanship that was subsequently transmitted in regular stages of descent was the Nen-ryu and it dates from around the year 1350. There was an earlier style, the Chujo-ryu, that went back to the end of the previous century but there is no positive evidence that the descent was regular or systematic.

The first half of the fourteenth century had witnessed a sharp decline in the military skills of the bushi in general. Matters reached such a pass that the third Ashikaga shogun, Yoshimitsu (1358–1408), gave full encouragement to the establishment of proper training in the military arts. Archery, swordsmanship, the use of the *naginata* (the curved-bladed spear), *sumo* as a military style of wrestling, the study of Chinese classical strategy, and so on, were all given an impetus. However, the almost incessant background of warfare between the unruly and politically ambitious military families provided the greatest incentive to the profession of arms, and men claiming special skills and with the ability to back these claims up could and did gain considerable prestige.

The art of swordsmanship was gradually equated with *heiho*, or tactics, and developed along two quite separate lines: *sen-ha kenjutsu*, or battle techniques, and *ryu-ha kenjutsu*, or the academic study of swordsmanship. The former comprised practical tactics for coping with the mêlée of the battlefield. The latter concerned the study of classical Chinese military philosophy as applied to such matters as strategy, tactics, and the principles of warfare, often in terms of combat between two swordsmen. The influence of the Chinese military philosopher Sun Tzu (*circa* 400 BC) has been great in all periods of Japanese military history right down to the present day. Modern kendo is the development of *ryu-ha kenjutsu*.

Towards the end of the fifteenth century and throughout the sixteenth century Japan experienced many wars as the central military government progressively lost control of its vassals. This period of almost incessant warfare is known as the Sengoku-Jidai,

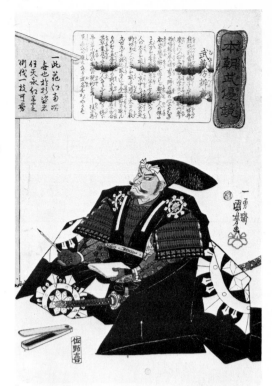

Saito Musashi-bo Benkei, the faithful retainer of Minamoto Yoshitsune at the end of the twelfth century. Print by Kuniyoshi. Victoria and Albert Museum, London.

心眼流

迅速をすれれをひ堂む

曲面之巻

top Minamoto Yoritomo (*right*) meets his younger brother, Yoshitsune (*centre*). Benkei sits behind his young master (*left centre*). Print by Kuniyoshi. Victoria and Albert Museum, London.

above The beginning of the *tora-no-maki* (secret-teachings scroll) of the Shingen-ryu, a traditional kenjutsu school dating from the sixteenth century under the patronage of the Nanbu clan. The scroll seeks to give historical authenticity by connecting the school's origins with the mythical *tengu* (shown here), who were said to be skilful swordsmen. Roald Knutsen collection.

right A scene from the Toho film *Yojimbo*, showing a *ronin*, or masterless samurai, attacked by a group of young townsmen.

the Age of War. Many schools of swordsmanship were developed, some of which were of major significance to the later development of kendo, and we have many well-authenticated records of the most famous swordsmen.

One of the greatest was a man named Tsukahara Bokuden, a minor 'baron' from Eastern Japan, who studied swordsmanship at the famous Kashima Shinto shrine, where his adoptive father was a ritualist. He is recorded as having fought nineteen times with the live blade, man to man, taken part in thirty-seven regular battles, and fought several hundred bokken matches. The *bokken* is a wooden practice sword, a very lethal weapon in expert hands. He died in 1571 at about eighty years of age and in his whole life he had been wounded but six times, all by arrows in battle! His first real-sword match was at the age of seventeen, when he killed his opponent. During his long life he is said to have killed more than two hundred enemies.

There is a record of a match fought by Bokuden against a swordsman, one Kajiwara Nagato. This must have taken place sometime in the first half of the sixteenth century. Nagato was an expert in the use of the sword-spear, the naginata, and it is recorded that his technique was so good that he could cut down in flight swallows, ducks, or pheasants. Despite this, his pupils were ill at ease about the impending match with Bokuden and urged their master to refuse the fight. Nagato replied:

There are always strong and weak things. It is due to an opponent's unskilled technique that I am able to cut both his arms with my spear. It is not so easy to defeat a skilled man armed with a long sword but my naginata is the same as a short-bladed spear, even if I am cut I will not die without defeating him.

This illustrates the philosophy of *ai-uchi*, or mutual striking down. Nagato knew full well that he was not better than Bokuden but firmly believed he was as good. Death meant very little to him; if he must die, then his opponent would assuredly be defeated too.

Forging a sword blade. Drawing for a colour print by Kuniyoshi. Victoria and Albert Museum, London.

Unfortunately he was no match for Bokuden. As soon as Kajiwara Nagato left his stool armed with his spear, Tsukahara Bokuden stepped in and with a single stroke cut the spear and the man in two.

Examining another recorded contest, we find that sixty or so years later kenjutsu had assumed other characteristics. Swordsmen were now studying applied psychology and adding this knowledge to their repertoire of lethal skill. A samurai of the Kyo-ryu in Kyoto had a match with a pupil of another school and defeated him. News of this fight spread rapidly and a student of Bokuden's style, Kashima Rinsai by name, immediately travelled several hundred miles to Kyoto to request a match with the victor, Mataichiro Naoshige. The match was arranged for sometime in June 1606.

Rinsai stood 6 feet tall and was armed with a very long spear with a curved blade known as a *nagemaki*. His opponent, the youthful Naoshige, had a real sword. As Rinsai edged forward, Naoshige said:

Rinsai! Tactics do not depend on our power alone. It does not matter if we fight with a large or small person. I am sorry but I will soon take away your life. You had better pray to Buddha.

In this way Naoshige forestalled his enemy by making him angry. Rinsai attacked violently but Naoshige avoided the rush. Then Rinsai tried to cut him by whirling his spear shaft. At that instant Naoshige jumped in close and cut down at the centre of his forehead. Rinsai fell and died a few days after the match.

Kendo today

Kendo is now practised with *shinai*, or bamboo swords, and wearing protective equipment. These changes were a product of the new concepts of swordsmanship that became current in the early Tokugawa period from about 1600 to 1750. The more mature and serious of the older ryu exerted the most influence, and the fact that Japan had now embarked on a period of increasing stability in which the military class was an anachronism brought about this change from kenjutsu to kendo. The term kendo now meant 'Ken-no-michi', the Sword's Path. It was a long and difficult road and it remains so to this day.

When a student comes to kendo for his first practice, he is told that we use three types of sword: the katana, the bokuto, and the shinai. In the days of kenjutsu the *katana* was the exercise weapon used to study in depth endless series of attacks and defences. As the student became more skilful, he studied techniques against a variety of different weapons, always depending on his master's skill. To test these techniques he used the *bokuto*, or wooden sword. To quote a sixteenth-century kendo maxim that is still in widespread use, 'A poor fencer comes in for hard blows.' The bokuto can be a lethal weapon even in non-expert hands. Towards the end of the eighteenth century the bamboo *shinai* came into common use for basic practice. This allowed a great deal of realism to be introduced into kendo since with the shinai and the wearing of armour there were comparatively few injuries. Nowadays the shinai is used first; later on there is study with the bokuto; and still later for certain theoretical practice the katana is employed.

In kendo the practice halls are known as *dojo*. Although this word is in common use throughout the martial arts, it was first used in kenjutsu many centuries ago, originating from the Buddhist term for 'a place of enlightenment' probably in the eleventh or twelfth century. Within the dojo, training is hard and sustained, following a varying routine under the watchful eyes of the senior ranks. In proper kendo the training is always hard and must be so. The accent is on discipline since it is only through the sometimes harsh feudal methods that we can reach the ultimate goal of the masters—mastery of oneself.

We use the word '*reigi*' to describe the discipline or etiquette of kendo. It is this reigi, or good manners and respect between kendoka at all levels, that is the most unique and valuable thing that kendo can offer the modern world, and it is as old as kendo itself. In a Western environment it would be impossible to impose a totally Japanese culture on our students and we do not attempt this. But in any dojo the students, Japanese or not, can observe the traditional kendo reigi and this encourages the growth of a fundamental understanding of the art that is naturally coloured by the individual's own cultural background. One of the values of kendo training, according to many masters, is that it produces a calm mind and allows its followers to face everyday problems squarely.

An aspiring kendo student must never forget that he is joining a society whose training programme dates back to very ancient military practice and whose members are conditioned to accept rigours in this training not for their own sake but for the moral values that lie behind them. For the greatest part of its history kendo or kenjutsu was practised almost exclusively by the bushi. To the warrior, perseverance, skill-at-arms, breadth of character, steadiness, and self-control in all situations were the goals that lay at the end of a lifetime's study of swordsmanship. These are still the aims. The swordsmen who founded the great ryu were often able to exert a significant influence on political thought and action. They were men who commanded an enormous esteem amongst

Early kendo armour. The upper equipment dates from 1751 to 1771; the lower armour from 1789. Line drawing. British Kendo Renmei.

A nineteenth-century kendo match taking place within a sumo ring. On the left is Ogawa Kiyotake and his opponent is Akamatsu Gundayu. Seated nearby is Sakakibara Kenkichi. All three were noted nineteenth-century swordsmen. Print by Kuniteru. Roald Knutsen collection.

their contemporaries and posterity; even today kendoka are highly regarded in Japan. It is for these reasons that kendo reigi is considered so important and is so closely observed within the dojo.

At the beginning the student must practise hard in order to reach the physical level required, but rapidly he realizes that he must develop his mental control in order to master apparently simple techniques. As a young man the ratio of physical kendo to mental kendo should be 90% to 10%; in middle age 50% to 50%; and in advanced age 20% to 80%. Therefore it is possible to start kendo training at any age from early childhood to advanced maturity; there is kendo to suit all conditions, even severe physical handicaps that otherwise rule out any strenuous exercise. Kendo can be practised throughout life. The will to continue regular training is the essential element in learning kendo.

There are four deep-rooted mental or intellectual problems to be overcome in kendo. These are fear, doubt, surprise, and confusion; they are known collectively as the 'Four Poisons of Kendo'. By resolutely confronting these problems with many opponents, the student tries to attain a calmness of mind in which every situation is perceived with equal clarity and he can look objectively at his surroundings. Only in this state of mind can he achieve the intuitive action necessary to strike an opponent effectively. Such a degree of mental training must be of benefit in all aspects of living.

Kendo, therefore, as opposed to kenjutsu, is not practised in order to destroy opponents but rather to train oneself in character building. In this aim of spiritual awakening kendo has much in common with Zen Buddhism. However, kendo is deeply influenced not only by Zen but by orthodox Buddhist, Confucian, and Christian philosophy.

The expert manipulation of the sword is only the means to the end. In a kendo match only one person may win but many people may take part. Physical prowess and technical skill are counted less important than doing everything with full spirit, the taking part even without hope of winning. What is important is attaining mental and spiritual calm and balance.

To practise kendo successfully implies a balance of body, brain, and intellect. This is expressed by the famous kendo maxim 'Ken-Tai-Ichi', which literally means 'Sword and Body as One'. The challenge of kendo is an intensely personal one; basically it is a question of whether the student has the determination to see his study through to the end.

Kendo equipment

The kendo student requires a certain amount of specialized equipment, all of which has been developed in recent centuries from the normal day-to-day clothing or armour of the bushi.

For practice the novice wears a lightweight cotton *keikogi*, or jacket, that is white with criss-cross black stitching. The *dan* or instructor ranks, known in kendo as *yudansha*, wear a heavier or hand-made quilted keikogi that is usually black or navy blue in colour. This jacket is tucked into the wide pleated trousers called *hakama*, the traditional formal outdoor garment of Japanese gentlemen. The hakama is usually black or dark blue. Rank cannot

This is an unusual and rare nineteenth-century armour made of wadded leather with shoulder flaps and long *kote*, or gauntlets, a considerable advance on the earlier equipment; on the opposite page, a high-quality modern set of armour.

top left A good general shot showing a kendo group in *chudan-no-kumae*, or middle position, with *shinai*, or practice swords, ready for *suburi* or basic practice.

centre left General practice, or *keiko*, at the Butokukan Kendo Dojo, England. In the foreground one student is making *shomen*, a straight cut at his teacher's head.

left Kendo practice-cutting, or *uchikomi*. This is the basic method of studying various techniques.

above One of the most difficult cutting techniques is that of striking the left *do*, or breastplate. In this picture the shinai is just about to strike the opponent but the movement will be directly away from the camera to the opponent's left rear.

above right Kendo *keiko* or general practice.

below right *Nito* against *itto*, or two swords against one sword. Here the long sword is attacking the raised left wrist of the swordsman on the left.

be distinguished by coloured belts as in judo or karate; an onlooker in the kendo dojo can only say with reasonable confidence that those wearing black and white keikogi and dark hakama are below 1st dan, while those wearing one-colour jackets and trousers are yudansha. In a very few dojo the yudansha wear all-white clothing but the norm in kendo is all dark.

Kendo *bogu*, or armour, has gone through several very interesting stages of development since the mid-eighteenth century, when it was first thought advisable to protect certain areas of the body in order to achieve more realistic training. At first the armour was constructed of bamboo sections laced together with leather or silk braid and was naturally closely derived from true armour. For kendo exercise it was only necessary to protect the front and sides of the trunk, the wrists and hands, and the head, so by the early nineteenth century the bogu was quite similar to that manufactured today.

The first part is the *men*, or face mask. This has a strong steel grill to protect the face and heavy wadded padding to soften the heaviest blows given by the shinai. The second part is the *do*, or breastplate, constructed chiefly of heavy strips of bamboo covered by stout leather which is lacquered to give a highly polished surface. The do is often beautifully decorated on the leatherwork and the lacquer. Thirdly we have the *kote*, or gauntlets, again made of leather and tightly wadded padding. Lastly comes the *tare*, an apron defence to protect the stomach and hips. Old kendo armours of the last century sometimes had the tare attached to the do.

A general-practice action shot of nito against itto. The short sword is used to block or deflect, the long sword to cut.

There is still amongst kendo students the warrior tradition that fine feathers do not necessarily make fine birds. Below 6th dan, kendo students may own and wear very expensive handmade armour but this should be quite restrained and conservative in its decoration and colouring. Black usually predominates with just a touch of richness in the braiding on the chest parts of the do and the 'beard' of the men. Very senior kendoka often wear beautiful armour with speckled lacquer breastplates and other magnificent decorative parts. This is in accord with their rank. For a junior to wear such armour would be presumptuous.

The order in which the bogu is put on is as follows. First the tare is secured round the waist, the wide *himo* or ties being knotted beneath the front flap so that the loops are out of the way during practice. Then the do is settled comfortably on the chest, with its himo being crossed to opposite shoulders at the back. Next the student puts on a light cotton towel called either a *tenugui* or *hachimaki*, the latter term being an older word meaning literally 'a helmet wrapping'. This acts partly as an additional pad beneath the inner men padding and partly to prevent perspiration from running down the kendoka's face into his eyes during hard training. Then the men is firmly tied into place and, once secured, the long side-flaps are twisted a little forward so that they stand proud of the neck and shoulders and the men is more comfortable. Lastly the kote are pulled on, the left one first and then the right.

All the armour is put on and adjusted from a kneeling position, a strong kendo discipline, on the principle that this is military equipment and in former times it was very difficult to put on real armour when standing and without assistance. If, during practice, any of the equipment needs to be adjusted or re-tied, then the student must do this from *seiza*, or full kneeling position.

The last and most important piece of equipment is the shinai, or practice sword. As we have already noted, three swords are used in kendo: the live blade, the bokuto or wooden sword, and the bamboo shinai. The practice sword is constructed of four

below A cut at the left wrist at the end of the Fourth Form of the Eishin-ryu *Tachi-uchi-no-i* Kendo-kata. The Eishin-ryu kata contains some ninety techniques of iai and kenjutsu that illustrate the theory of this particular style. It originated in the sixteenth century.

below right A thrust at the chest in the *Tsuke-komi* form of the Eishin-ryu Kendo-kata.

opposite above right An unusual posture from the Eishin-ryu: a variation of *jodan-no-kamae*.

opposite left From the First Form of the All-Japan Kendo-kata. The All-Japan Kendo-kata, formulated earlier this century, comprises a standard ten sword-forms that illustrate a number of basic principles.

opposite below right Facing camera is *uchidachi* (the attacking sword) about to be cut by *shidachi* (the countering sword) in another part of the First Form of the All-Japan Kendo-kata.

well-seasoned matched lengths of bamboo with special leather mounts held tightly in place with a waxed cord. The shinai has a fair amount of give in it so that it can absorb the considerable shocks that it must sustain during training or contest. A well-maintained shinai, and they should always be kept in good order, may last its owner two years or more but generally speaking it is thought to be an expendable item.

There is as yet no absolute standardization in the length of the bamboo sword, but there are minimum weights laid down for tournament kendo. Most children use a light shinai between 34 and 36 inches in length. Adults use 38-inch or 39-inch shinai but even here there are many exceptions.

The targets in kendo
Since modern kendo has developed from the academic ryu-ha kenjutsu, and not the drastic free-for-all of the battlefield, the number of valid areas for cuts or thrusts is limited quite severely. They are as follows:
1. *shomen* a vertical cut delivered to the centre of the forehead
2. *hidari-men* an oblique cut at the left temple
3. *migi-men* an oblique cut at the right temple
4. *migi-do* a downwards cut at the right side of the breastplate
5. *gyaku-do* a similar cut at the left side of the breastplate (rarely used)
6. *kote* a cut at the right wrist or lower forearm
7. *hidari-kote* a cut at the left wrist or lower forearm but only valid if the arm is raised to shoulder height or higher
8. *tsuki* a thrust at the throat to strike the 'beard' of the men

The novice learns to cut these precise targets one by one until after a time he can pick out and cut accurately any required area. In no way does this lead to a formalization that reduces kendo's

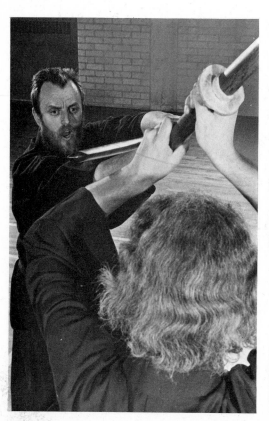

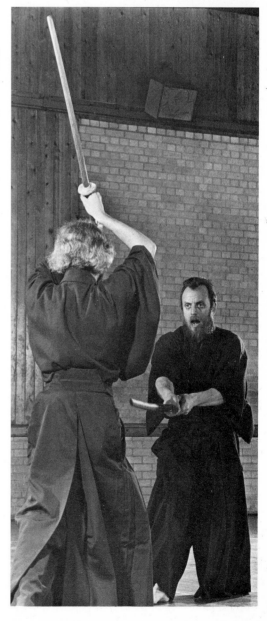

effectiveness as a fighting system; on the contrary the trained swordsman can cut any part of his opponent without the slightest hesitation. Quite simply these are the targets that will best render an opponent *hors de combat*. In contest kendo all the targets are of equal value and a successful cut will score one point.

Whether a cut is made in practice or in contest, there are always certain basic requirements. The general posture must be correct; the cut must be delivered with the correct part of the sword; it must be accurately aimed at a specific target; there must be some movement of the feet; the shinai must not touch the opponent's sword close to the target; and there must be a kiai with the cut.

Kiai or shouting

One of the more important aspects of kendo training and yet one of the least understood is the use of *kiai*. This is the explosive sound 'made to inspirit oneself and to dispirit the opponent' as one kendo master puts it. To be full of kiai means to be physically, mentally, and spiritually alert from the top of the head to the tips of the toes. In such a state one cannot be attacked and a kendoka making an attack while filled with kiai will be irresistible.

In former times kiai was also known as *toate-no-jutsu*, the art of

opposite Three shots from the Fourth Form of the All-Japan Kendo-kata: the beginning (*above left*); a strong thrust at the stomach by the facing swordsman (*above right*); and the retaliatory cut at the head (*below*).

left Kendo students standing in armour, ready and waiting.

below A turning defence with the short sword against a head cut by the long sword, from Eighth Form of the All-Japan Kendo-kata.

Kendo training at the Nippon Budokan in Tokyo during the 1969 Children's Summer Training. This gives some indication of the enormous popularity of kendo in Japan.

striking from a distance. It takes two main forms and has two simultaneous effects, though only when fully mastered. The first form is the attacking sound, intense and sharp, made at the opponent on the instant the cut is delivered. Such shouts as 'Ei!' 'Ya!' are good examples. The second form is what can be termed a 'stopping' kiai; 'Ho!' or 'To!', broader-based sounds which are deeper but still intense, come into this category.

One effect of kiai is to create a momentary break in the opponent's smooth, controlled concentration. This slight break is caused by the noise shock acting on the auditory nerve from the ear to the brain, and the opponent cannot for that fleeting moment react to the attack. The kiai also causes a momentary break in the breathing rhythm, exactly in the same way that the sudden noise of a car back-firing causes one to start. Together the two effects give the accompanying cut every chance of success. The study of kiai is very difficult and to develop the proper sound so that it is not made in the throat takes a long, long time. Kiai is to have the body and mind in complete harmony.

In modern kendo the names of three of the targets – men, do, and kote (with the accent on the last syllable) – are also used in place of proper kiai. In this case the kendo student must make certain that the accompanying cut is aimed at the called target in order to score.

Kendo matches

Kendo *shiai* usually take the form of what are termed in kendo 'three-point matches'. The match time is usually set at 3 to 5 minutes and the first to score two points at time is the winner. If the score is one point to nothing at time, then the winner is the contestant who scored. Should the match be drawn, then either it is declared a draw or a time extension is fixed and the match continues until one of the contestants takes a point and is automatically the winner. The first properly conducted 'three-point match' took place as long ago as the end of the sixteenth century and many recorded instances have come down to us from the succeeding centuries.

In the dojo, and formerly at some official shiai, one-point matches are often held. To take the first point is the most important object for any swordsman because it signifies a moral victory whatever the subsequent result. In consequence one-point matches are frequently lively affairs with strong attacking kendo and cuts made with full spirit.

All too often present-day kendo takes on a very strong 'sport' aspect, especially at tournaments. An example of this is the common use of one-handed cuts that developed within university kendo in Japan in the period after the Second World War. Unless these cuts are very well executed they bear little relation to fighting techniques, and in kendo the cut made with the shinai must always be thought of in context with the real sword. Would the technique, if it were made with a live blade, cut and kill the opponent even if he were wearing armour? In 'sport budo' we frequently see techniques that have no proper relation to the original concept and can therefore only be condemned.

The purpose of shiai kendo is to give the student a medium in which he can test his training under conditions of external pressure. The contest is a series of actions, attacking and defending, that require uninterrupted concentration of mind. The match is ultimately decided by the difference in the mental power of the contestants.

There must be total harmony and co-ordination between the physical and mental actions. In fighting no-one can continue an offensive indefinitely and so there are always advances and retreats, attacks and periods of defence or collecting oneself for the next assault. It is a common fault amongst inexperienced kendoka that at the end of an attack sequence the fencer permits his guard to drop mentally and frequently physically. The development of *zanshin* or awareness is therefore an important objective in kendo training. Never be off guard for a single moment whatever the circumstances.

To succeed in kendo or any budo the student must be prepared to work long and hard: there is no easy way.

top   Kendo *suburi*, or empty-cutting exercise, at the Vectis Dojo in the Isle of Wight, England.

above   This is the Fourth Form of the All-Japan Kendo-kata taken at the World Goodwill Kendo Tournament in Tokyo, October 1967, in the presence of HRH the Crown Prince.

Iai-jutsu and iai-do

'Iai is in the scabbard, once the sword is drawn the rest is Kendo.' This is the definition given by a contemporary Japanese master but it may require some further explanation.

Iai-jutsu includes the many different systems of techniques for drawing the long, and sometimes the short, sword from its scabbard and in the same move using the weapon offensively against an opponent or opponents. It is also the study of how to return the blade to the sheath on completion of the movements without loss of *zanshin*, or awareness of the immediate situation. Once drawn, any further parries or cuts are properly within the realms of kendo, or kenjutsu, but the replacing of the sword by touch alone is certainly iai. In other words, we can practise kendo without knowledge of iai, but we cannot practise iai without some knowledge of kendo.

The origins of iai-jutsu are now completely obscured by time. We know that there were systems of drawing the sword that were either offensive or defensive as the situation merited as far back as the fifteenth century, but the originator of most of the modern schools is considered to be a *bushi*, or member of the warrior class, named Hayashizaki Jinsuke Shigenobu, who died at the age of about seventy-three in or around 1616. As with many of these master swordsmen, time has greatly embellished his deeds, but it is said of Hayashizaki Jinsuke that he had a gift for mixing easily with all classes of men—truly a rare quality for a proud samurai— and that it was his custom when travelling to ride on the back of a slow-moving ox.

By definition iai-jutsu technique makes full use of the ever-ready sword. Therefore every possible circumstance where iai may be required was envisaged and the student exercised until he had fully mastered each move. In the early years iai was a branch of kenjutsu and involved immediate action for attack or defence. As time went on, however, and the comparatively tranquil Tokugawa period ensued, many masters saw in iai an excellent means to develop mental and intellectual disciplines, hence iai-do. In the nineteenth century one leading master said of his style:
Learning and study alone are not enough. Without hard study and making of techniques yourself (that is, until your hands and mind move as one; until you can think automatically and unconsciously)

you cannot master swordsmanship. There is a high goal—the stage of unification of spirit and technique.

In iai the student performs all his practice alone. The techniques are extremely varied and are made from crouching, sitting, reclining, standing, or walking postures. Every angle of attack is studied—left, right, front, or rear— and in darkness as well as daylight. External hazards are sometimes introduced, such as a narrow space not wide enough to accommodate the sword on a normal sweep out of the scabbard, or a low obstacle above the swordsman which he must remember while dealing with a life-and-death combat situation. There are also techniques to be employed against another iai exponent and forms against enemies who try to prevent the sword being drawn by grasping the hilt or the scabbard from front or rear.

The student usually starts his iai training with a basic series of forms or *kata*. Nowadays the most popular style is the Omori-ryu Iai, comprising eleven forms, which was developed in the late seventeenth century from the Eishin-ryu Iai. All but one of these forms commence from *seiza* or full kneeling posture, the only exception being a walking iai named *Koranto* or Tiger Stalking Sword. The seventh form is a direct survival from feudal times, the technique to be used by a swordsman acting as second to a man committing *seppuku* (hara-kiri). This cannot be truly said to be an iai technique yet it is still contained in the Omori-ryu Iai. A student will commonly practise the first form only for up to two years, though this will vary from master to master. Some prefer to give their pupils a wider basis on which to build.

In Omori-ryu Iai all the forms are practised with the greatest possible emphasis on physical control, smooth movement, mental and spiritual balance. Indeed one is left with the impression that the immediacy of fighting has largely been stripped away. This is a particular characteristic of do techniques as opposed to the older jutsu forms. However, this style does teach great discipline and the fundamental requirements of the art.

The older, parent style, the Eishin-ryu, was originated by one of the pupils of Hayashizaki Jinsuke. Until 1868 this style and the related Omori-ryu remained a secret of the warlike Tosa clan. In this school, with its four separate series of kata as well as six kenjutsu kata, we can see several very old drastic techniques of pure swordsmanship. The sense of menace is very strong and in some of the forms there is not one but several enemies to be met and destroyed.

'When we draw at first the sword movement is slow, then faster, and finally the cut at the enemy is like the wind.' So said the modern kendo master Tanaya Masami, *Kyoshi*. In iai there is always a superb concentration, a striving after perfection. Since all the forms are practised solo, it is of the greatest importance that the student thoroughly understands the real meaning of each part of the kata. This is not just theoretical or academic practice; it must be real. A famous swordsman of the eighteenth century said that if we merely practise kata as form then our action will be as meaningless as that of performing marionettes; we must practise kata with full spirit. Iai-jutsu is pure theatre. The opponent, although

The late Muto Shuzo *Hanshi* 9th Dan demonstrates Omori-ryu Iai in his Tokyo garden.

top Turning in *Hasso-no-kamae* in the *Ryu-to* (Flowing Sword) form of the Omori-ryu Iai. This shoulder position derives from the wearing of the real-armour helmet, which prevented the sword from being used above the head.

above Iai-do practice under the late Muto Shuzo *Hanshi* at the Old Mitsubishi Dojo in Tokyo. The five students are all masters of 7th dan or above!

above right Cutting down obliquely to the right front in one of the forms of the Eishin-ryu Iai dealing with swordsmanship in confined areas or against multiple opponents.

opposite Sonoda *Hanshi*, a member of the Japanese Upper House of Parliament, demonstrates a method of returning the sword in the Omori-ryu Iai.

imaginary, must really exist, actually be seen by the swordsman.

There are four areas of study in all iai techniques, whether we are considering jutsu or do forms. These are the *nukisuke*, or drawing move; the *kiritsuke*, or cutting action; the *chiburui*, or shaking of blood from the blade before returning it to the scabbard; and the *noto*, or sheathing of the sword. In order to master these aspects so that all actions are performed with effortless ease while in a state of zanshin, many iai masters make their students practise using only live blades. It is quite true that practice using a replica *iai-to* (*to* is a sword) or a *bokuto* (a wooden sword) has nowhere near the same psychological effect as a razor-sharp blade passing within a hair's breadth of one's hand or body. The constant danger to the careless rapidly brings improvement to poorly executed technique and with serious daily practice the iai student soon acquires polish.

It is important to realize that iai-jutsu is not in any sense a sport. The forms of iai require long and serious study to perfect – iai-jutsu is truly warrior art. Iai should never be practised without the benefit of initial teaching from a master.

Kyudo

To find the origins of *kyudo*, the art of archery, one must reach back into Japan's past. The country's medieval chronicles abound with stirring tales of the military struggles of those troubled times and of the famed samurai warriors involved in the conflicts. Such men, redoubtable heroes like Minamoto-no-Tametomo and Nasu-no-Yoichi, all had one thing in common, a legendary skill with the bow.

The Kamakura period of the twelfth to fourteenth centuries was an era of inter-clan struggles between Minamoto and Taira, and Hojo and Ashikaga, and also of two attempted invasions of Japan by the Mongols. In such times the mounted archer, a samurai of rank, reigned supreme, forming the élite fighting arm of any military force. The warriors of the northern and eastern provinces, renowned for their fighting prowess, were in fact known as those skilled in *Kyuba no Michi*, the Way of Bow and Horse. Those proud, unruly warriors studied amongst other skills the art of *kyujutsu*, the techniques of battlefield archery. Their aim was to achieve complete mastery of the weapon. Spiritual training was not then a feature of their teaching, although at a later date Zen Buddhism began to exert a great influence on the samurai's life and attitude towards death.

The feudal warfare and power struggles of the Middle Ages saw the origins of many famous *ryu* or schools of archery. Probably the most influential in terms of modern archery were the Ogasawara-ryu and the Heki-ryu. Ogasawara Nagahide founded his ryu of archery and etiquette in the fourteenth century, and it was naturally a style suited to the predominantly mounted warrior of that period. Ogasawara's teachings are in fact still demonstrated each year in a colourful display of mounted archery, the famed Yabusame ceremony at the Kamakura Hachiman shrine.

The Heki-ryu, however, was a later development, originating in the sixteenth century. A more functional form of archery designed for the foot archer, this style was much more suited to the large infantry battles of the infamous Sengoku-Jidai period or the Age of the Country at War, when for a hundred years Japan was totally engulfed in civil wars.

However, during the same century the wholesale introduction of matchlocks in the hands of low-rank warriors was to spell the end of the archer as an essential part of the army of a *daimyo* or great noble. A company of musketeers could be trained much more quickly than a company of archers and its weapons had a more devastating effect. The enforced peace of the following centuries under the all-seeing eye of the Tokugawa shoguns furthered the decline of kyujutsu and the other martial arts. By the late eighteenth century the once exclusive weapon of the proud samurai could be seen used by the common folk at archery booths in city streets. Only in the court and temple were the old traditions of archery continued. It was from the aesthetics of the court and the spiritual disciplines of the temple, coupled with what remained of the old ryu, that kyudo evolved.

Kyudo was developed as a non-violent alternative to the military art of kyujutsu. It places the emphasis not on killing with accuracy but on spiritual teaching and on unity of mind, body, and bow. Self-discipline and perfection of technique are of more importance in kyudo than actually striking the target. It is here that one can see the influence of philosophies such as Zen.

Kyudo equipment

Although kyudo is now a peaceful study, the traditions and materials used are all direct links with the past. The great samurai long bow of the twelfth century and the samurai clothing, consisting of a light jacket, or on formal occasions a *kimono*, and the *hakama*, or large baggy breeches, so traditional to the martial arts, are still used. Kyudo is very much history in a living form.

The Japanese bow is a composite weapon constructed of bamboo sections glued together side by side. The back and belly are covered by strips of bamboo, and pieces of wax wood cover the sides. Its average length is over 7 feet and it varies in thickness from $\frac{1}{2}$ inch to 1 inch, depending on the strength of draw required. The average bow has a 40-pound to 50-pound pull but a teacher's bow can draw as much as 90 pounds. Arrows are in proportion to the bow and at least 39 inches in length. If their user has long arms, thus pulling a longer draw, the arrows can obviously be much longer. They are made of bamboo cane, heat straightened and polished, with large 5-inch flights bound on. The heads are very similar to those of Western target arrows.

To a Western archer the most unusual aspect of kyudo is that the arrows are shot from the right-hand side of the bow and that the bow itself has its grip not in the centre but one third of the distance from the bottom. This is probably a relic of its origins as a cavalry weapon. The Japanese bowman, in common with other oriental archers, draws the string with his thumb, not the fingers, so a deerskin shooting-glove is worn, with the thumb reinforced and lined with bone. No bracer is worn on the left arm as the techniques used allow the bow to revolve in the hand on release.

The dojo

As a rule kyudo is practised indoors and the traditional Japanese *dojo* or practice hall has one completely removable wall which allows direct access to a garden, on the other side of which is the target mound under its own pavilion. The bowman fires from the dojo and sends his shaft winging across the garden to its target, a

An incident from the twelfth-century Gempei wars. Minamoto-no-Yoshitsune and a small band of followers descend the hazardous Hiyodori Pass to attack Taira forces encamped at Ichi-no-Tani. Scroll painting on silk by Kyushin. Victoria and Albert Museum, London.

opposite above A page from the early nineteenth-century work *Hokusai's Sketches from Life*, showing samurai both training and hunting with bow and arrow.

opposite below One of the legendary feats of Nasu-no-Yoichi. The Taira fleet taunt the Minamoto forces by raising a fan above one of their ships. On Yoshitsune's orders Nasu-no-Yoichi rides into the waves and with one arrow strikes out the rivet securing the fan. Print by Kuniyoshi. Victoria and Albert Museum, London.

left An archer firing a humming-bulb arrow in a court archery ceremony. Such arrows were traditionally used to open battles and sometimes in ceremonies to dispel evil spirits.

below left A *sensei*, or master, demonstrates an ancient form of archery, shooting from the squatting position. This requires great control and iron leg and stomach muscles!

below A boy of samurai stock practising archery. His training mount stands in the background with a youthful attendant. (Such wooden horses are still used today.) Print by Kunisada. Victoria and Albert Museum, London.

very tranquil experience during the summer but requiring all one's self-control and discipline at 7 am on a winter's morning. A kyudo target is very simple—plain white circles on a black background, offering no scoring incentive, only a focusing point. For the usual range of about 33 yards the target diameter is 15 inches. For open-air shooting in Japan, however, the range is increased to 90 or 100 yards and larger targets are used. In this country kyudo is practised in halls or gymnasiums as a good wooden floor is essential to training. Otherwise traditions follow the Japanese pattern as closely as possible.

As explained previously, court and temple influence is very obvious in kyudo. This manifests itself in the many traditional formalities and customs of the art, all of which help to encourage a measure of self-discipline and control. Different styles or teachers have their own minor variations in technique and custom, although there is a standard method recommended by the All Japan Kyudo Renmei, the organizing body in Japan.

Firing a pair of arrows

The actual practice of kyudo involves shooting a pair of arrows with perfect technique and control. This sounds simple but novices may only just approach it once or twice in their first few years of practice. Firing a pair of arrows can best be explained as a series of basic positions or moves.

The archer always opens and closes any shooting performance by bowing. In this way he pays respects to the dojo. He then stands side on to the target with the bow in the left hand and two arrows in the right hand. The tip of the bow touches the floor and the hands are at the hips. The bow is lifted to a vertical position at eye level and an arrow is fitted and nocked. The second arrow is also placed on the bow and held parallel to the first but in reverse with the flights towards the target. The bottom of the bow is then placed on the left knee in a more relaxed position, and the second arrow is lifted off and held in the little finger of the right hand by the hip in readiness for the second shot.

Next, all the energies have to be focused into the lower stomach, the centre of gravity, in readiness for shooting. The string is grasped with thumb and two fingers, and the bow or left hand adjusted in preparation. The student must attempt to force his gaze into the centre of the target, thus projecting his 'self' and therefore the arrow into his objective. Once relaxed and settled, the archer turns his head to face the target squarely and raises the bow above the head.

With the arrow horizontal at all times he then partly draws the bow by pushing towards the target with the bow hand, until the bow is about one third drawn. From this position the left hand continues to push forward, co-ordinating with a circular pulling movement of the right hand.

At full draw the arrow is at mouth level, the string is drawn to well behind the ear, and the body is completely relaxed and balanced. This position is held until the arrow is involuntarily released. If grip, control, and technique are correct the bow will fly round, striking the outside of the arm with its power expended.

The archer finishes in a cruciform stance, his power gone with the arrow but still in a state of *zanshin* – an alert but relaxed awareness, contemplating his actions. With the firing completed, the student lowers his hands to his hips and the tip of the bow to the floor, ready to shoot the second arrow. Obviously a demonstration of kyudo *kata* or formal kyudo has many added frills and flourishes. The actual shooting is made more difficult due to the fact that kata always starts and ends in *seiza* – the sitting-on-the-heels position so difficult for the Western student.

The philosophy of Kyudo

Difficult as it may be to understand, kyudo is not archery in the accepted sense, although it can be studied as such. It is rather a form of meditation (a much misused word I dislike using) in which the bow and arrows are only aids to study. Kyudo teaching aims at making bowman, bow, and target as one through concentration of mental and physical forces. The bowman is then in complete 'oneness' with the universe, actually shooting at himself whilst aiming at the target. The act of shooting must be effortless, almost without purpose. Concentration on technique or on striking the target will only hinder progress along an already difficult path.

A famous saying used by Japanese masters is 'It shoots', 'It' being the bow. Thus it is the bowman's spirit or soul which shoots the arrow, not the conscious act of the bowman. The true bowman is at one with nature and rid of the 'self' that hinders us in our everyday actions. This all sounds very involved. In training one is told to concentrate yet relax, to gain perfect technique yet not to think of it while shooting. By concentrating on the one point (the target) and relaxing physically, by trying to ignore the conscious act

opposite above left The late Anzawa 10th Dan Hanshi, displaying perfect technique and control at full draw. Anzawa sensei was instrumental in introducing kyudo to Britain.

opposite below A lady archer having just released her shaft displays *zanshin*. Note the relaxed body but still alert expression.

opposite right An elderly sensei practising kyudo in a traditional setting. This picture illustrates well the traditional Japanese kyudo dojo.

The six stages in firing an arrow: the opening stance; the arrow on the string; raising the bow; the bow at half draw; full draw; and zanshin.

of shooting but still having control, one can with much practice achieve true kyudo. Human nature being what it is, at this point one's troubles start again. The student begins to think 'so that's how it is done' and attempts to repeat the action. 'It' is no longer shooting. The archer's proud 'self' is back in control; so back to square one. This is, I suppose, what kyudo is: the age-old struggle of man's fight with his own spirit.

Words can never adequately describe the philosophy or techniques of any martial art. Because of its strong emphasis on spiritual training, this is particularly true of kyudo. It is far better to visit a dojo, watch the training, talk to the students and teacher, and then form your own impressions. To quote a famous kyudo saying: 'Better to see once than to hear one hundred times.'

There are no barriers of age or sex in kyudo. It obviously has appeal for women and the not-so-young because it is slower and less physically demanding than other martial arts such as judo or kendo. It can be studied purely as a hobby or in its deeper aspect as a method of controlling, developing, and improving one's spirit and character. There are only a small number of people outside Japan who study kyudo, its lack of competition being hard for many people to understand. In Japan, however, it has about 450,000 practitioners, although this is still a small number compared to the millions of judoka or karateka in that country. British kyudo is actively encouraged by the All Japan Kyudo Renmei and individual masters, who assist with advice and equipment and the occasional instructional visits.

Naginata-do

opposite A lady of samurai rank defeats and restrains an armed intruder. Women were often expert with both sword and spear. Print by Kunisada. Victoria and Albert Museum, London.

Naginata-do is a form of spear exercise that is still widely practised today. It is one of the most ancient of the Japanese martial arts, dating back to the earliest beginnings of the warrior classes in the seventh and eighth centuries AD. It is, therefore, fully as old as swordsmanship and the art of archery; it may even be older than the former since Japanese authorities date the oldest regular school of naginata technique back to 1168 whereas the earliest sword school is thought to have been founded in 1350.

In these ancient times the *naginata*, or curved-bladed spear, took several forms. The most common one had a socketed or tanged blade some 36 inches or more in length. The shaft was always stoutly banded and longer than the blade. A second form was the *nagemaki*, a heavy, very long sword blade mounted on a shorter sturdy shaft. Both weapons were very popular with warriors, especially in the turbulent monastic armies of the eleventh and twelfth centuries and increasingly so with the warrior class, or *bushi*, from the twelfth to the fifteenth century.

Gradually the character of warfare changed and military fashion favoured the straight-bladed *yari*, or spear, as a lighter and more effective weapon against the sword, both on foot and on horseback. The large-scale use of infantry during the Onin War (1467–77) finally established the yari at the expense of the naginata and the use of the latter soon became limited to certain religious sects and to ladies of the bushi class, as a household weapon. It is with the latter group that the modern, post-1600, use of the weapon is chiefly associated and nowadays naginata-do is widely taught on the curriculum of girls' schools and colleges in Japan, especially in the west. A naginata-do federation has recently been formed in the USA and the art is followed to a limited extent in Europe.

Like kendo, naginata developed many different schools in its long history—425 to be precise. Many of these were inter-related with other martial disciplines, especially kenjutsu and yari-jutsu. The oldest was the Ko-ryu but perhaps the most famous were the Tenshin Shoden Katori Shinto-ryu (the Heaven-revealed Divine Style), the Jiki-Shinkage-ryu, and the Tendo-ryu.

The techniques of these schools were often materially different and probably much more drastic than the modern style, which in the main is practised by women. There are only a few men, often of

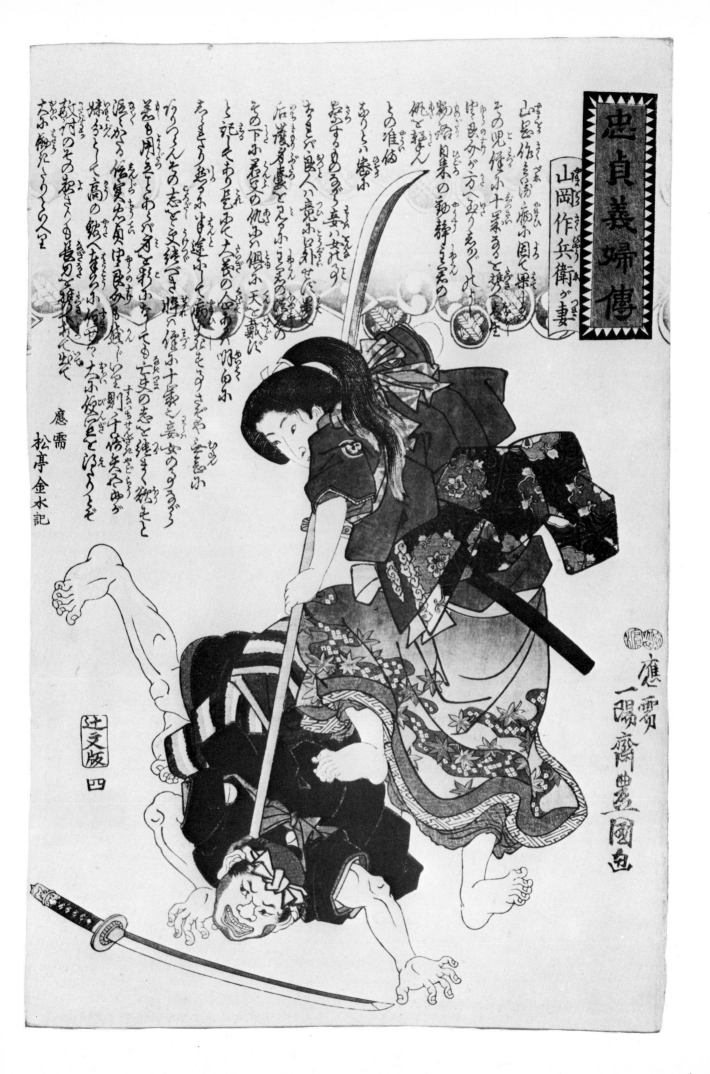

A spirited impression of naginata from horseback. Print by Yoshikazu. Victoria and Albert Museum, London.

Naginata practice is largely based on repeated basic techniques in the same way as for kendo. In this picture the lady facing the camera has commenced a cut at *sune* (the shin) and this is countered by a side *men* or head cut.

opposite   Three naginata versus kendo shots. The top left-hand picture indicates very well the intensity of the aggressive action of the naginata. The swordsman is concerned mainly with defence, with only a chance of delivering his own attack. In the top right-hand picture the naginata has just cut the *men* of the swordsman while he is preparing to strike, and the lower picture is a very good action shot, showing a cut at the *suneate* (shin guards) by the spear.

The Jiki-Shinkage-ryu. Naginata versus kendo demonstrated by Mr and Mrs Sonoda, both *Hanshi*, using live blades.

advanced kendo rank, within the art. Like other tradition-conscious martial arts, several of the older systems are still preserved in private *dojo* or halls that are extremely difficult to locate, let alone enter.

In early centuries the naginata or nagemaki was wielded in strong arcs, often with the intention to maim the enemy's horse before dealing with the fallen rider. Naginata-jutsu required great stamina in order to swing the heavy weapon along accurate interchanging curves, making the fullest use of the blade, the shaft, and the vicious iron ferrule at the butt. The technique of rapidly whirling the weapon was known as *ha-kaeshi*. Some of the terms still used in naginata are evocative of these ha-kaeshi techniques. We have, for example, the *Mizu-guruma-gaeshi* (Waterwheel Cut), the *Kazu-garuma-gaeshi* (Windmill Cut), and the *Cho-gaeshi* (Butterfly Cut).

Ha-kaeshi, coupled with the greatly increased distance from an opposing swordsman, gave the spearman a very real advantage. Since the naginata is essentially a slashing spear using open lines of attack (those outside the body width), counter-attacks can only be effectively made as the swing commences. The swordsman must close the distance by rushing into the attack. The root of the problem in fighting against the naginata is not the techniques that are employed by the spearman, though these are important. It is more the extreme *ma-ai*, or interval, that forces the swordsman to fight at a distance approaching twice the normal. If the naginata is wielded at a speed equal to normal sword technique, the swordsman must move at almost twice this speed to close the distance and cut effectively. Thus practice against an expert *naginata-ka* can be very exhausting. The swordsman has to time the exact moment to attack; he must always be on the alert and ready to rush in with his

50

cut. Conversely the spear can be used to create a chance for a devastating counter-move against an over-eager opponent.

Modern naginata under the aegis of the All Japan Naginata-do Federation is usually *Atarashi-Naginata*, literally a New Style of Naginata. Practice is nearly always spear against spear, using the comparatively light *keiko-naginata* with a curved bamboo blade constructed on similar lines to the kendo *shinai*. The practice spear is usually about 6 feet 8 inches in length but longer shafts are recommended for taller students. The protective armour is exactly the same as that used for kendo, but with the addition of the *suneate*, or shin guards, as a defence against strong sweeping cuts below the knee. Sometimes the *kote*, or gauntlets, have a separately padded index finger to give extra sensitivity to the spear posture.

The valid targets in naginata are just the same as for kendo but with the addition of the *sune*, or shins. The same conditions for cutting apply; that is to say the cut must be delivered with intention to strike that particular area, it must be given with proper form, it must be made with the correct part of the bamboo blade, it must be accompanied by a *kiai* or shout, and there must be movement of one or both feet simultaneous to the strike. However, in naginata the cut is usually comparatively light compared to that given in kendo. If the spear were a real weapon, its weight would ensure the cut was effective.

While kendo is possibly too physically hard for the majority of girls or women, naginata presents a reasonably safe yet strenuous exercise that through its long circling movements and great control teaches excellent posture and deportment. Long reach permits ladies to practise against swordsmen on more than an equal basis.

A demonstration of old naginata versus kendo forms for the Tokyo Metropolitan Police some years ago. The spear is a *kata-naginata* made of oak. Note the women have their sleeves tied back.

Yari-jutsu

The use of the straight-bladed spear is the one major system of the warriors' art that has not taken on the more formalized and intellectual *do* form. Kendo, iai-do, naginata-do, and kyudo all underwent profound changes during the period of Tokugawa government (1615–1868) and through to the present day. Kendo has even been debased in part to a sport form, though fortunately the older and more traditional thinking still remains very strong. But to this day the techniques of handling the straight-bladed spear remain as drastic and suited to the battlefield as they were to the end of the Age of War (1612).

The spear, and by this term we mean the *yari* as opposed to the curved *naginata*, is an extremely ancient weapon throughout the world. In Japan the first references to the spear go back to the myths surrounding the creation of the Japanese islands, and the straight-bladed spear has ever since played an important part in Japanese combat.

Although spears have survived from the eighth century AD, it was not until the large-scale wars of the Onin period towards the end of the fifteenth century that the yari appeared in great numbers on the field of battle. But after the Onin War it is said that no fewer than 450 martial-arts *ryu*, or schools, included yari technique amongst their *kata*, or series of formalized training techniques. Until firearms were introduced to the battlefield in the mid-sixteenth century, the yari vied with the sword as the most popular weapon.

It was in the late fifteenth and early sixteenth centuries that two of the greatest warrior experts emerged. The first was Iishino Choisai (died 1488), who founded the Tenshin Shoden Katori Shinto-ryu (Heaven-revealed Divine Style), in which the sword, the yari, and the naginata are given prominence. This ancient style is followed to the present day. Choisai is regarded as one of Japan's greatest spearmen, both with yari and naginata. The second, and one of Choisai's many pupils, was a general of the Kashima clan, Matsumoto Bizen-no-kami Naokatsu. Kendo historians acknowledge the latter as one of the truly great swordsmen in all kenjutsu history, a master of *to-so-jutsu*—sword and spear. It is to this man that the invention of the cross-bladed spear called the *magari-yari* is reliably credited. During his active lifetime—a period of incessant warfare—he fought in twenty-three battles, his favourite weapon being the yari, and he is reputed to have taken over one hundred heads. Though Matsumoto Bizen-no-kami was a brave *bushi*, or member of the warrior class, and was immensely skilled in all the arts of war, he died in 1525 of a spear thrust to the stomach received during a minor night battle at Takamagahara in Shimosa. This small-scale affair, scarcely bigger than a skirmish between a few hundred men, took place when Lord Kashima Yoshimoto made a night attack in an effort to recover his lost fortress. Matsumoto Bizen-no-kami was fifty-seven at the time of his death. His Lord, Yoshimoto, also fell in the fighting.

By the middle decades of the sixteenth century, the *tanegashima*, or matchlock, was beginning to dominate the major battlefields. One of the generals of the warlike Takeda clan, whose lord was an ardent follower of the principles of the Chinese classics on warfare, was Yamamoto Kansuke Yorinori, also known as 'One-eyed Yamamoto'. He, too, was famous for his to-so-jutsu and it is related that he practised cutting water in flowing streams, thus giving to the name of his personal style, Doki-ryu. During his career, however, he followed the Kyo-ryu of the Kyoto region, and was 'most successful in capturing castles and forts and in increasing his lord's territory'. He was killed in action in August 1561 by matchlock fire.

Generally speaking the yari was not ideally suited to the small-statured Japanese warrior. The majority of spears that have survived have shafts between 7 and 9 feet in length. While longer spears were certainly used, and they are recorded up to an enormous 22 feet, the smaller ones seem more typical. The yari is generally lighter in weight than the naginata and more effective in use, great experts excepted. With the longer-bladed varieties the chief techniques were based on thrusts and cuts made from oblique angles or on rising or falling lines. The shorter-bladed yari were primarily used for *tsuki* (thrusting) or from horseback. The primary target areas were the groin/stomach and the chest/throat regions.

The *su-yari*, or long straight-bladed spear, was frequently used from horseback as this famous incident from the story of the forty-seven ronin shows. Some of the loyal forty-seven Ako retainers are here crossing the Ryogoku Bridge in Edo (now Tokyo) on their way to their dead lord's family temple, Myokoji, when they are met by an official and advised to change their route to avoid publicity. Print by Kunisada II. Victoria and Albert Museum, London.

Spear training sketched by Hokusai in the nineteenth century. This practice spear has a padded head made of leather.

opposite above Tsuki, or thrust, in yari-jutsu. Note the powerful action backed by the whole body-weight.

Two yari-jutsu ready postures: (*below*) *Yari-hiza-no-kamae* or the crouching posture; and (*opposite below*) *Seigan-no-kamae* or the basic posture.

Kasumi-jodan-no-kamae with the su-yari, a very typical aggressive high posture with the spear.

above right *Ha-kaeshi*, the whirling technique, with the *nagemaki*. The nagemaki is similar to the naginata but the blade is heavier and longer than the shaft. This particular weapon has a blade 43 inches long.

The redoubtable Toyotomi Hideyoshi, who rose in supreme power after the murder of his lord, Oda Nobunaga, in 1582, once demonstrated the tactical use of the long spear (which was over 10 feet) against the short spear, and this parallels accounts in classical Chinese treatises on the theory of warfare. At least one modern kendo master has stated that in his opinion yari-jutsu is probably the most effective form of hand-to-hand combat, firearms apart.

To conclude, here is an anecdote from the great repository of reliable kendo history which goes by the name of *Shigemasa's Night-time Tales*. The event took place in 1588, and illustrates how to win matches by fair means or foul.

The originator of the Ten-ryu was a bushi named Ide Hangan Denki-bo, who, in his youth, had studied under the famous Tsukahara Bokuden (died 1571). He spent a period in the Kamakura Hachiman shrine before announcing his Ten-ryu or Heavenly Style. His fame grew in Hitachi province in Eastern Japan but his success caused the follower of another kenjutsu school, one Kasumi-no-suke, to become jealous and spread slanderous tales about him.

Eventually Denki-bo offered to settle this matter with a real-sword match and, as Kasumi-no-suke was his inferior, the latter was cut at once and lost his life. When the news of his death reached his

father, O'kuma-no-kami, he became very angry and complained of the matter to his master. Makabe Anyaken was also angry and commanded him to challenge Denki-bo to a match. Kasumi-no-suke had been a favourite pupil of Anyaken's school and Anyaken felt honour-bound to avenge him, especially since Denki-bo lived within his territory. The offer was accepted and Denki-bo decided that the match should take place at the Acala shrine in Makabe.

On the day of the match, Denki-bo waited with only two pupils at the appointed place. O'kuma-no-kami arrived with several retainers armed with bows and with many foot soldiers, or *ashigaru*. But seeing Denki-bo standing in the centre of the shrine grasping a *kama-yari*, a spear with a sickle-shaped blade, O'kuma-no-kami hesitated, impressed by Denki's dignified bearing. At length he called out that he had heard Denki-bo had a secret technique for cutting down flying arrows known as *Ya-kiri-no-tachi* and he asked to see this. Denki agreed and changing his spear for a magari-yari he cut down three successive arrows shot at him. Then, at a signal from O'kuma-no-kami, his retainers all shot arrows at Denki-bo as fast as they could. Denki-bo whirled his yari and cut down or deflected as many as possible but at last he was hit and died.

Kasumi-chudan-no-kamae with a nagemaki, a middle position from a secret technique devised to hide the intention of the spearman.

above left   The start of a left oblique cut with the nagemaki.

Okinawan weaponry

opposite   A block against a sword cut with the nunchaku held crossed.

The chains of islands that lie to the east of the Asian landmass start at Taiwan and extend in a north-easterly direction up to the Kurils in the North Pacific. The central and most important group forms the islands of Japan but to the south, bordering the China Sea, is the chain of islands known as the Ryukyu, the chief of which is Okinawa.

For many centuries the Ryukyus have formed the stepping stones, so to speak, for cultural influence between South East Asia, China, and Japan. They were a refuge for many of the defeated Japanese Taira clan in the twelfth century and subsequently came under political control from Japan for long periods of their history. Japanese government in the Ryukyus was characteristically severe and in the early seventeenth century a law was introduced proscribing the possession of weapons.

Against this background of foreign repression, the peasantry secretly developed Chinese combat styles that increasingly became distinctly Okinawan as the years passed. Okinawan-*te* (hand fighting) eventually became known as karate-jutsu and is dealt with in the karate section of this book. However, the te masters were able to broaden their styles with the introduction of a limited number of weapons, none of which is indigenous to the Ryukyus but which finds its origins in South East Asia. These weapons are all basically farm implements with the exception of the *sai*. Their association with karate is limited to those styles that are of Okinawan origin.

The rokushakubo

This Japanese word means 6-foot staff; a *shaku* is approximately 1 foot and a *bo* is a staff. The rokushakubo is a hardwood staff that tapers towards either end, varying in diameter from 1 inch to 2 inches. The use of this weapon is entirely dependent on a sound knowledge of te technique, though there are parallels here with native Japanese *jutsu* or martial-arts methods with staves.

Many years must be spent in mastering the handling of the bo before attempting combat. Like most long-shafted weapons, it is best operated on outside or external lines of attack in thrusting or striking. When used on interior lines it is not so efficient but can be employed effectively in blocking or tying up the opponent while te techniques are applied.

A block with the nunchaku, followed by a kick to the opponent's side (*below*).

The kama

This is the rice-harvesting hand sickle which has a short blade set at right angles to a hardwood handle that thickens towards the butt end. It is an implement that can be found all over Southern Asia and Japan. For combat purposes it sometimes took the upgraded form of a *kama-yari*, a spear with a hooked blade, and it is related to the *kusari-gama*, a sickle attached to a weighted length of fine chain.

The weapon was used either singly or in pairs entirely for close work, where it could slash, hook, rake, chop, deflect, or block in a wide range of basic combination tactics. With the increasing sport orientation of modern karate the use of the kama is fast dying out and its survival is limited to a few *kata* or training forms using wooden practice weapons.

The ton-fa or tui-fa

This curious domestic implement, used as a handle to turn the hand-operated millstone when grinding rice, is a tapered hardwood billet between 15 and 20 inches in length with a short projecting side-handle set about 6 inches down from the thicker end of the billet.

When employed as a weapon, the user holds the handle loosely but firmly to allow for the maximum manipulation of both ends. With the short or long end lying along the underside of the forearm, the tui-fa permits very effective punching or striking, as the opposite end is employed to jab with devastating force at unprotected vital points. The weapon is also used to block cuts or blows in a manner dictated by te technique. Like the kama, it can be effectively used in pairs.

The nunchaku

The use of this innocuous-looking weapon made of two equal lengths of hardwood hinged by a short piece of silk cord or chain is typically Okinawan. Nunchaku are common as plain agricultural grain flails all over Southern Asia and larger versions used to be found in Europe, but under the severe dominance of the Japanese the islanders developed the weapon as a subordinate branch of the te styles of combat.

Here again, the size of the weapon dictates that it must be employed in close fighting, always from te postures. It is first whirled in a fast figure-of-eight or zigzag fashion before the opponent with the object of disturbing the composure and gaining the mental initiative. The free hand carries out the normal te movements of blocking or defending and, as the chances occur, the nunchaku delivers smashing blows to the face, the hands, the wrists, the knees, the shoulder-blades, or the ribs. Alternatively or in combination with such attacks, the weapon can thrust at the several other vulnerable parts of the opponent, such as the throat or groin, or, when really close, it can strike at the kidney regions of the back. One particularly effective technique is to crush the opponent's hand or fingers between the two pieces of wood, leaving no choice but to give in.

Like the other very specialized weapon systems, the nunchaku

Striking the opponent's face with the sai after blocking a sword cut.

is fast vanishing from correct usage – despite the frequency of its appearance in kung-fu films.

The sai

This is a weapon which occurs all over South East Asia from India to Okinawa. Difficult to define properly, the sai is sometimes known as a short sword, but it is, in fact, closely related to a trident. A hand weapon with a central 'blade' between 15 and 20 inches in length and two forward-curved quillons, the butt end of the hand grip terminates in a pronounced pommel. The whole weapon is made in one piece of solid iron weighing up to 3 pounds. Although the Japanese have been familiar with the trident and even this basic sai for much more than a thousand years, the weapon never became part of the classical tradition and remained so far as we are concerned within Okinawan-te.

In order to improve the hand grip under conditions of stress, many sai users bind the 'hilt' with strips of cotton material over a wound-cord base. Often two or three sai were carried, one in each hand, and the possible third thrust into the waistband in reserve.

Originally the sai was a formidable weapon, easily able to kill or maim an enemy either by striking or thrusting or even as a missile. Now the use of the sai is restricted to the Okinawan karate systems and its sharp points are blunted and smoothed out. However, its manipulation requires a very high standard of training and skill. To be really effective against a good spearman or swordsman, the sai user must himself be expert in the use of the spear or sword otherwise he cannot hope to defend and counter these major weapons successfully.

When we look at the use of the sai it immediately becomes apparent that this is in no way a short sword. It falls within the category of a double-armed truncheon and its techniques are entirely subordinate to Okinawan-te. In the hands of an expert, the sai can be employed to block cuts or blows delivered by sword, polearms, or unarmed attacks, either by a normal grip with the quillons forward or by a 'snap-back' action that reverses the central 'blade' back along the underside of the forearm with the butt-end forward. As in all true combat, defence is never enough to gain the victory, and the sai can be used most effectively as a formidable weapon of offence, by both poking and thrusting or by ensnaring the opponent's weapon in the prongs, even disarming him, while kicking or striking blows are delivered to parts of his unprotected anatomy.

In Japan the only similar system was the use of the *jutte* by the *bushi*, or warrior class. The jutte was about the same size as the sai, though with only one projecting arm. Primarily a weapon to assist in the restraint of armed criminals, especially those carrying swords, its techniques could easily be adopted for offence and it is said that it developed from the use of the short sword. The jutte first appeared on the Japanese scene in the sixteenth century and the possible inventor of the original system was Miyamoto Muni-no-suke Kazusada, the father of the famous swordsman Miyamoto Musashi. Kazusada, a high-ranking warrior, probably died in 1591, though the sources are confusing, but it is certain that he practised the art of arrest in addition to kenjutsu, and that the use of the jutte was secondary to his swordsmanship. It is interesting to note that Kazusada went up to Kyoto in the mid-1580s and fought a *bokuto* or wooden-sword match with Yoshioka Kempo of the Kyo-ryu, Kazusada winning by two out of three points. This is the first recorded *sanbon shobu*, or three-point match, since then an important feature of fencing combat.

The above comments on jutte-jutsu in the Japanese islands serve to illustrate the value of an expert knowledge of swordsmanship as a basis for using the lesser weapon. It is interesting to speculate on how the Okinawan fighting men became proficient in the use of the sai when an intimate and profound grounding in swordsmanship was denied them under the severe prohibition of weapons, especially swords, by the Japanese authorities. It is of course possible that the sai was introduced to the te repertoire on a purely theoretical basis. The style of sai techniques in the Okinawan systems certainly bears little similarity to short sword, jutte, or stick movements in Japan. A pre-requisite for training with the sai is several years' thorough grounding in karate-do based on Okinawan principles.

Blocking a sword cut with the sai.

Unarmed Combat

Sumo wrestling
Jeffrey Somers

Ju-jutsu
Paul Crompton

Judo
David White

Aikido
Jim Elkin

Karate-do
Bryn Williams

Sumo wrestling

A few years ago there were photographs in most of the English papers of a gigantic Japanese man in Great Britain on his honeymoon. Dressed in traditional style, he went with his bride to a well-known London restaurant and ordered his meal twice through. He was a *yokozuna* or sumo grand champion.

Most people who know something about Japan will have heard of the giant wrestlers but few know why these men need to be so fat or that their sport is called sumo. In any form of grappling a low centre of gravity is more stable than a high one, and the *sumo-tori's* enormous weight helps to develop the tremendous force they need – hence the large stomach. They achieve their massive stature through the Japanese art of *haragei*, abdominal development or the 'soul in the stomach', and the average weight of a sumo fighter is 286 pounds. One famous champion, Dewatage, was 6 feet 7 inches tall and weighed 484 pounds! It is also interesting to note that most top sumo-tori come from fishing families of the south or farming families of the north; very few come from the towns.

Sumo is perhaps the oldest of the Japanese martial arts and evidence of its practice goes right back to the *Nihon Sho-ki*. One of Japan's oldest chronicles, written in the eighth century AD, it mentions a sumo contest as having taken place in 23 BC. In the ancient form, the purpose was to cause one of the opponents to surrender unconditionally and killing was permitted. Sumo was not a general skill possessed by the warriors for use in combat but was employed only by chosen fighters representing various sides in a dispute. The use of such formalized single-combat often avoided massed confrontations and undue bloodshed.

In time, a religious element came into sumo and fights were staged as an oblation to the gods in exchange for divine protection. During the Nara period, sumo was patronized by the imperial family, as it still is; the present emperor is a sumo fan. Unfortunately, Japanese etiquette prevents him from staying till the best bouts at the end of the tournament because this would make him look greedy. Emperor Shomu (701–756), a famous patron of Buddhism and the builder of many temples, is also reported to have included some sumo among the traditional games and celebrations of the harvest-thanksgiving festival held in the month of August. Wrestlers attained special social status and many were appointed as guards to the court.

In the Heian period sumo became popular as a spectacular sport and Emperor Nimmyo ordered that it be regarded as a symbol of the nation's military strength. A little later in this period the *bushi*, or warrior class, began to use it for combat. In the Kamakura period the military class transformed sumo to full battle effectiveness. Emphasis was placed on the gaining of skill in grappling from a standing position as well as in taking an enemy to the ground and holding him helpless. With the enemy subdued he could either be restrained for capture or he could be killed, usually with the sword.

Kumi-uchi or grappling, as this form of battlefield combat became known, is a type of sumo applied against an enemy, however dressed. Clad in the lightweight armour which had been developed from the tenth century, the warrior could not be moved or even gripped as easily as an unarmoured warrior. The methods of kumi-uchi involved offensive techniques based on strong legs and hips, which enabled the warrior to close with an enemy and throw him to the ground.

Gradually, during the Azuchi-Momoyama period, sumo began to be developed as a sport and professional wrestlers seem to have made their first appearance at approximately the same time. Available records indicate that in 1623 Akashi Shiganosuke requested and was granted permission by the military powers to hold public wrestling-matches in Edo with professional sumo-tori. His example was followed by the priests of Kofukuji in Yamashiro, who were authorized to hold wrestling bouts in order to raise funds for the construction of a temple. Such practices were encouraged by the military leaders of the period, who even employed teams of wrestlers in their own mansions. In time, sumo matches became full-fledged tournaments. During the Edo and the succeeding Meiji periods, sumo became very popular, revolving around the yokozuna, who became rather like modern film-stars and commanded nation-wide respect.

Nowadays there are six *basho* or grand tournaments each year and these take place as follows:

January   Tokyo
March   Osaka
May   Tokyo
July   Nagoya
September   Tokyo
November   Kyushu

Each one lasts for fifteen days and ends with the presentation of the Emperor's Cup. Every day starts with contests between young fighters, followed later in the day by the senior fights. This main section is made up of contests between the top fifteen sumo-tori divided into the following grades:

mae-gashira literally, 'before the head'
komusubi junior champion, 2nd class
sekiwake junior champion, 1st class
ozeki champion
yokozuna grand champion
All of the above meet each other, and their final score is out of fifteen.

A sumo-tori in the ring. Most prints showed heroes, famous beauties, or famous actors in their outstanding roles. Sumo was so popular that the famous fighters were also depicted. Print by Kunisada. Victoria and Albert Museum, London.

Sumo contests

A sumo contest takes place in a circular ring about 10 feet in radius called a *dohyo*. Its edge is marked by straw bags, and the surface of the ring is covered with smooth earth. The two fighters wear only *mawashi*, a type of loin-cloth with a long fringe of strips, or *sagari*, at the front. Each fighter tries either to push his opponent out of the ring or get his body to touch the ground.

When two contestants face each other, their expression and attitude give some idea what their attack, or *tachiai*, will be like, but paradoxically it is both somewhat unexpected and always exciting. They are like two mountains coming towards each other, and many of the fighters' professional names end in *yama*, the Japanese word for mountain.

The bouts are supervised by a referee called a *gyoji*, who is dressed in a kimono made of silk and in the samurai style. He also wears a special court hat. There are five judges outside the ring to help the referee with difficult decisions.

It may be no exaggeration to say that, in all sport, there is no more brilliant spectacle than the triumphal entry of the grand champions. Termed the *dohyo-iri*, this takes place every day of each fifteen-day tournament. About 3.30 pm when the minor bouts, which have been going on since early morning, have ended, the *yobidashi* or announcer steps into the arena and beats two pieces of wood together. The ring is carefully swept, and one half of the top-ranking wrestlers stride in single file down the aisle leading to the ring. They are clad in beautifully embroidered *kesho-mawashi*, or aprons of multi-coloured brocade. Every wrestler has his patron, and these aprons are given by them. A good-quality apron can cost £750 (US$ 1730); some wrestlers have so many they can wear a different one each day of the tournament.

The wrestlers step into the ring and form a circle round it, clap their hands in unison, hitch up their aprons half an inch or so, and then withdraw by the same route as they came. The remaining half of the top-rankers then march down the opposite aisle and go

A fight during a basho. Print by Kunisada. Victoria and Albert Museum, London.

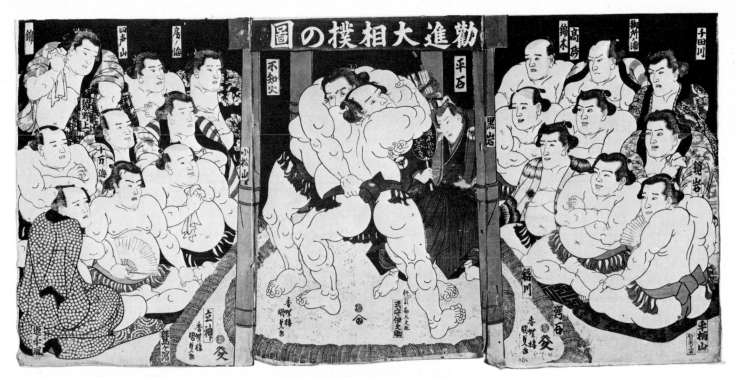

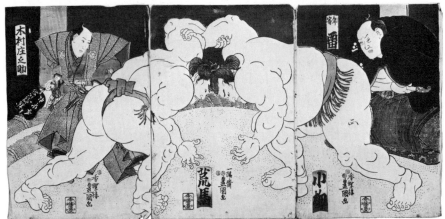

above   A wrestling match so famous in its time that it was commemorated by a special wood-block print or *ukiyoe*. Print by Kunisada II. Victoria and Albert Museum, London.

left   This fight is being refereed by Shonosuke Kimura (*left*), whose family still provides referees. Print by Kunisada. Victoria and Albert Museum, London.

A modern auditorium. The canopy over the ring is similar to the roof of a Shinto shrine.

Dohyo-iri, the triumphal entry of the grand champions.

A set of *kesho-mawashi* for the Grand Champion Wajima and his bearers, given by his fan club.

A grand champion performing the dohyo-iri ceremony with his *tachimochi*, or sword bearer, and assistant or *tsuyuharai*. The referee, or *gyoji*, is in the foreground on the right.

Shikiri-naoshi or getting in tune to fight.

through exactly the same motions in the tournament arena.

Then comes the ceremonial entry of the grand champions. Amid applause from the supporters, a referee follows a clapper-beating announcer down the aisle. Next comes the first grand champion's *tsuyuharai*, or attendant. Then the great man himself and finally, bringing up the rear, his *tachimochi*, or sword-bearer.

Led by the referee, all four participants in the ceremony step up into the ring. The yokozuna, flanked by his retainers, squats down and then, after rising and bowing to the gallery, marches to the centre of the arena. He balances himself on one leg and brings the other down with a loud thump to the ground.

All this done, the grand champion retires to the edge of the ring, bows once more, and withdraws with his attendants, his place to be taken by the remaining grand champions in turn. When all have gone through the ritual, the announcer again beats his clappers to attract the gods' attention and the breath-taking spectacle is over. The fight can begin.

Following an initial flexing of muscles and stamping of feet at the edge of the ring, the rivals pick up a handful of purifying salt, scatter it, and squat down facing each other at a respectful distance in the centre of the arena. The referee keeps a watchful eye on them. In the course of this ritual, which is known as the *Shikiri-naoshi*, the contestants get down almost with their noses in the earth, pound the floor with their fists, and fix each other with piercing glances. The ceremony is limited to 4 minutes, during which period the rivals march back and forth about four or five times between the centre of the ring and 'salt corner'. When time is up, the time-keeper nods to one of the young attendants sitting by a water pail. He in his turn stands up and nods to the contestants and to the referee.

A bout may be won either by ejecting one's opponent from the ring or by getting him down inside the arena. In the former case it spells defeat if so much as a toe is over the edge; in the latter a tilt is lost if any part of the body above (and including) the knee hits the floor. The winner may achieve his objective by any one of sixty-eight recognized techniques known as *kimari-te*. The word is almost impossible to translate for a man may be thrown, pushed, pulled, flipped, tapped, etc., either down or out.

There are, naturally, certain things that are taboo in sumo. For this is not all-in wrestling by any means. It is forbidden to strike a man with the fists. And the karate chop, delivered with the side of the hand, is also prohibited. Hair-pulling and eye-poking are not allowed; neither is slapping the ears and grasping the throat. A wrestler may not kick his opponent in the abdomen, chest, or head, and lastly, care must be exercised so as not to lay hands on the *mae-tatemitsu* – that part of the grappler's attire which sweeps down at right angles to the abdomen and covers the vital organs. Violation of any one of the above ensures automatic defeat.

By the end of the *Shikiri-naoshi*, the preliminary posturing, the wrestler has – or should have – made up his mind whether he wishes to come to grips or not. Certain wrestlers invariably prefer not to do so. They like to slap their opponents towards the edge of the ring and then, when they have them right off balance, push them out

The salt ritual, an ancient purifying ceremony.

Tsuppari, a series of hard slaps to drive one's opponent out of the ring.

opposite left   Three swift manoeuvres. Hataki-komi (above). The technique of stepping aside and pushing one's opponent out of the ring. Ketaguri (centre). As the opponent rushes in, his legs are taken from under him. And Ashi-tori (below). The opponent's leg is grabbed and held on to until he loses his balance.

opposite right   Three grappling techniques. An example of Yori-kiri (above), showing the moment of defeat. Yori-taoshi (centre), an exciting variant of Yori-kiri, in which both fighters fall out of the ring together with the man on top the winner. And Uttchari (below). In this tackle the fighter by the rope, almost defeated, suddenly twists and throws his opponent out of the ring, following him a fraction of a second later.

of it. The slapping manoeuvre, which is known as Tsuppari, is a most valuable weapon in a wrestler's armoury. It enables him to polish off his man extremely quickly. A sumo tournament lasts fifteen days and is an immense drain on a fighter's energy. If, however, he can get through a bout in about a second, it is like a day's rest. The average time required for a match is about 10 seconds. Very few go on for more than a minute.

For those who do not wish to grapple, slapping is not the only manoeuvre. There is, for example, Hataki-komi, which usually requires not more than a second to execute. A man senses by the look in his opponent's eyes just before clinching that the latter is intent on getting the fight over quickly, so he simply steps to one side and gives his rival a hefty smack on the back as he flies past.

Another quick manoeuvre is Ketaguri: as an opponent rushes in, his legs are kicked from under him (time required: 1 second). Or Ashi-tori, grabbing one's rival by the leg and keeping him hopping around the ring until he finally topples over.

Now for the grappling types of sumo. The initial object is to get a firm grip on an opponent's mawashi or belly-band, thus gaining some control over his movements. The latter will try to prevent this, either by wriggling about or by keeping the lower part of his body at a safe distance. There are also some wrestlers who are open to criticism for repeatedly having their belly-bands loosely tied so as not to afford their opponents a secure grip. Once a hold has been secured, a period of jockeying for position ensues. Using his tremendous weight, a wrestler may gradually edge his opponent towards the edge of the arena and gently march him out. This tactic, known as Yori-kiri, is the most common of all. A more thrilling variant is Yori-taoshi, in which victor and vanquished go

hurtling out of the ring together, with the former on top. Timing, in this as in all sumo moves, is of the utmost importance. A skilful wrestler bides his time until he can catch his rival off balance and then launches his attack. He grasps his opponent's mawashi firmly with both hands and runs him around until he is off balance, finally hoisting him high in the air and out of the ring. Then there is *Uttchari*. This occurs when a man, on the point of being toppled out, digs in on the edge of the ring, hoists his rival up over his stomach and, with a quick turn, flings him out, following himself a tenth of a second later.

The *Uwate-nage* and *Shitate-nage* are beautiful throws by which lighter men often overcome much heavier opponents. The former may be translated as the 'Upper-hand Throw', the latter the 'Under-hand Throw'. In the *Uwate-nage*, the throw is executed with a hand outside the other man's arm; in the *Shitate-nage*, with a hand inside it. More often than not quite a lot of manoeuvring takes place and several fruitless attempts are made at a throw before an opponent is finally caught off balance and flung down.

The above description includes some of the techniques most commonly seen. But there are countless variations, depending on exactly how a man is thrown, pulled, pushed, slapped, kicked and so on, either down or out.

Each day fights are concluded by a chosen fighter performing a short ceremony with a bow called *Yumitori-shiki*. This recalls sumo's connection with military history whereas some rituals indicate a close involvement with Shinto more than with Buddhism. In its early days tournaments were often held in the grounds of Shinto temples and even inter-village bouts were held so that the winner would bring good luck to the harvest of his village.

The grand tournaments of sumo are rather like the cricket test-matches in England or the World Series of baseball in America. The best sumo-tori have large fan-clubs and even companies shower gifts on them. Until recently the sport has been only for Japanese but now tournaments are staged in Hawaii and on the American mainland. Takamiyama, a current star, is the first non-Japanese to enter professional sumo. He comes from Hawaii and, although of Japanese descent, is technically an American citizen. Could this be the start of foreign success in a traditional Japanese martial art such as we have seen in others? Only time will tell.

Sumo throws: *Uwate-nage (above)* and *Shitate-nage (above left)*.

opposite Takamiyama, the Hawaiian sumo-tori, at shikiri-naoshi.

The *yumitori-shiki*, or bow ceremony, closes each day's fight during a basho. It is said to commemorate a sumo tournament held in Azuchi Castle to celebrate a victory by the famous war-lord Oda Nobunaga in 1575. An unprecedented prize of 500 *koku* (1 *koku* equals 4·96 bushels) of rice was offered to the winner, who was also given a bow. It is said that this same bow is the one being used for this particular ceremony.

Ju-jutsu

In other sections of this book you will find descriptions of sumo and judo. In sumo the combatants are more or less naked. In judo the clothing simulates normal peace-time wear. Unarmed combat techniques have depended to a large extent on what a man is wearing, and the history of ju-jutsu is closely related to this sartorial point.

Sumo wrestling was performed as early as the eighth century AD and influenced the *kumi-uchi*, or grappling, techniques of the warrior, clad in armour, who found himself in a close-combat battle situation. Perhaps deprived of his weapons, thrown from his horse, or seized in such a way that he could not deliver a weapon blow, he needed a method of freeing himself, incapacitating his enemy, and tying up his captives for ransom. Gradually there emerged various masters of kumi-uchi, and in time schools, or *ryu*, were formed, the empty-hand styles being referred to as 'yawara' and later, in the eighteenth century, 'ju-jutsu'.

In its early form ju-jutsu was primarily concerned with empty-hand combat in battle, belonging to the *bujutsu*, or martial art, forms of Japanese combat. Not until much later, when peace reigned, did various more aesthetic forms of ju-jutsu emerge which inclined more to *budo*, or martial ways. It was Jigoro Kano, the founder of modern judo, and his successors, who continued this refinement to a point where the lethal and crippling techniques of ju-jutsu were eliminated and a sport, in the modern sense, emerged. There is therefore an enormous gulf separating the death-dealing ju-jutsu methods of early Japan, and the kind of conception commonly held by most Westerners, based on books such as *Textbook of Ju-jutsu* by S.K. Uyenishi.

There are theories claiming that ju-jutsu came from China. However, the Ancient Chronicles of Japan recount how in AD 712 Tatemi Kazuchi threw a certain Tatemi Nokami 'as if throwing a leaf', and in the *Nihon Sho-ki*, AD 720, it is also related that Nomino Sukume killed a sumo wrestler with a kick. Writers point to these two incidents as evidence of early empty-hand methods in Japan and say that one need not look towards China.

Leaving controversy aside, one finds that most ju-jutsu ryu were also associated with one or more weapon techniques. The empty-hand methods therefore supplement the weapons virtually as a reserve or complementary weapon. The earliest of these schools is said to have been Daito-ryu Aiki-jujutsu, founded by General Shinra Saburo, in the twelfth century AD. The *daito* is a 39-inch-long sword, carried by the samurai. The second oldest ryu was the Take-no-Uchi-ryu, founded in 1532. Prince Takeuchi is supposed to have learned the techniques in a dream. Since that time, every head of the ryu has borne the name of Takeuchi. The famous Yagyu-ryu was founded by the adopted son of Japan's most famous swordsman, Miyamoto Musashi, by name Araki Mataemon. He also combined grappling with the use of weapons. Chinese influence is apparent in the history of the Kito-ryu of ju-jutsu; a Chinese dignitary named Gempin introduced some grappling arts to three Japanese *ronin*, or masterless warriors, who then proceeded to found the Kito-ryu. Ratti and Westbrook, two modern writers on the martial arts, trace the influence of this school in the *Koshiki-no-kata* of Kodokan Judo, an advanced form of judo training simulating the techniques used when fighting in armour. A full description of the different ryu could fill several books.

What of the words 'ju' and 'jutsu'? The 'ju', as in judo, means 'compliant', 'yielding'. It is often translated as 'soft' but that is misleading; in this context 'soft' does not mean 'weak'. As Donn F. Draeger, an expert on Japanese martial arts, has pointed out, great strength was sometimes needed to perform a ju-jutsu technique. It is the way in which the technique is performed which is 'ju' or 'compliant'. Ju uses the force of the opponent to overcome him; ju adds the force of the opponent to one's own force. Ju-jutsu can be aggressive as well as defensive. *Atemi*, the art of attacking the vital points of the body, can be used for defence or offence. The word 'jutsu' links a fighting method with the *bugei*, or martial arts of war, not with sporting or aesthetic purposes. So, ju-jutsu really means 'yielding martial art', a martial art incorporating the use of the opponent's force.

In the corpus of jutsu techniques we find striking, kicking, strangling, choking, locking, throwing, holding down, immobilizing, bending joints, and resuscitation of an unconscious or seemingly dead person. There is also the esoteric method of killing with a shout known as *kiai-jutsu*. Masters of this art are said to be able to utter a cry in such a way that an opponent is paralysed or killed.

The vital points of the body used by ju-jutsu students in attack or defence are the same as those employed in karate, kung fu, and other oriental martial arts. It goes without saying that these were also targets for weapon attacks. Some, but not all, of these points were also used to revive unconscious persons. Knowledge of the vital spots and resuscitation techniques are connected with acupuncture methods. Records also exist showing that prisoners of war were sometimes used as guinea-pigs for experiments in this field, just as condemned men were used for testing the cutting power of prized swords.

Physical fitness was a pre-requisite for successful ju-jutsu, and some ryu advised a strict moral and dietary régime for reaching perfection in the art. Withdrawal to a Buddhist or Shinto shrine often figures in the history of the masters of ju-jutsu, so it is apparent that the influence of the *boshi*, or monks of Japan, has been felt in the different ryu.

Ju-jutsu joint-locks illustrated in an old Japanese print. Just one of a variety of ways of immobilizing an opponent.

This print from the book *Tales of Old Japan* shows the practical use of ju-jutsu when dealing with an unfaithful wife and her lover. The wife receives a kick and the wrestler is about to be disarmed.

Most ju-jutsu masters were not averse to enriching their own styles by studying others. But, as in Chinese kung fu, secrecy was a hallmark of most styles. The reasons for this secrecy are plain. In combat the ability to spring a surprise technique is invaluable. One must also remember that in the early days the books which are now so freely available were non-existent. Only in the scrolls of the ryu were the techniques written down. Apart from that there was no information, except by word or imitation. Members were sworn to secrecy, and the scrolls were handed down from one ryu head to another.

It is important then, in looking at ju-jutsu, to remember two things. One, it is primarily a fighting method, useful in all situations and at all distances. Two, although this aspect has less significance in ju-jutsu than in most other martial arts, it can be used as a way of spiritual, mental, and physical well-being, incorporating a number of aesthetic and less practical techniques.

Ju-jutsu for self-defence
Ju-jutsu, as a fighting method, is of practical, daily interest to police forces the world over because they have to use methods of arrest and are frequently attacked by one or more assailants. In the USA in particular, policemen have found their training-programme organizers very open in the question of self-defence methods. Karate, kung fu, judo, marine hand-to-hand, ju-jutsu and other styles have all been welcomed.

It is worthwhile referring to the opinions of men trained for police

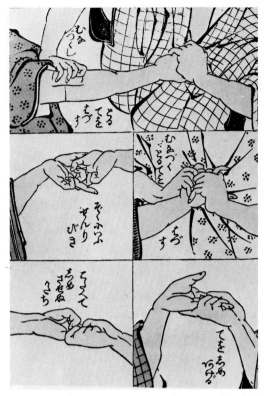

work because they have had to put their self-defence systems to the acid test. In the main, they seem to require three qualities:
1. a high level of fitness and strength
2. a well-developed and strong punch
3. a well-developed and strong, low kick

Throwing techniques, arm-bending, locks, and holds are considered of secondary importance. Speed, strength, and mobility seem to be the basic requirements. It is little use to be able to hold one man in an armlock whilst the other hits you over the head with a cosh. It is much more practical, if the situation demands it, to be able to knock an attacker out quickly, and be free to deal with his accomplice.

Robert K. Koga and John G. Nelson of the Los Angeles Police Department were teaching their system of defence and arrest to police trainees in the late 1960s. Their book on the subject, *Police Weaponless Control,* presents two perfect examples of what has just been under discussion:

1. A man tries to strangle you from the front, his arms outstretched. You grip one of his hands, twist outwards, and with your free hand you push him away.
2. A man tries to strangle you from behind. You swing your fist up and back to strike him as hard as possible on the nose. This will at least cause him to slacken his grip for a moment and you begin to turn and break free.

The first example is typical of the unrealistic presentation of ju-jutsu techniques frequently taught today. A strangle attack is never

above The famous Japanese woodblock artist, Hokusai, recorded examples of gripping techniques used by exponents of ju-jutsu.

above left A typical practical blow in ju-jutsu, in which the man on the right grabs his opponent's hair and pulls his head down with a quick jerk, at the same time driving his knee up into the face.

right and opposite below   Here the attacker applies a strong arm-lock which in combat could effectively disable at least the right arm. Carried further (*opposite below*), the shoulder could also be injured. The difference between the two positions is important and should be noted. In the first the victim can move his free arm, and even his feet; in the second he cannot.

below   A blow aimed at the point where the nose meets the upper lip. This blow with the edge of the hand can be very dangerous and is only advisable in cases of life or death.

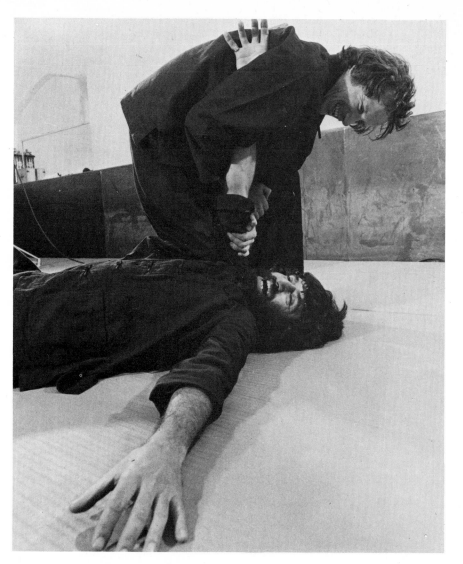

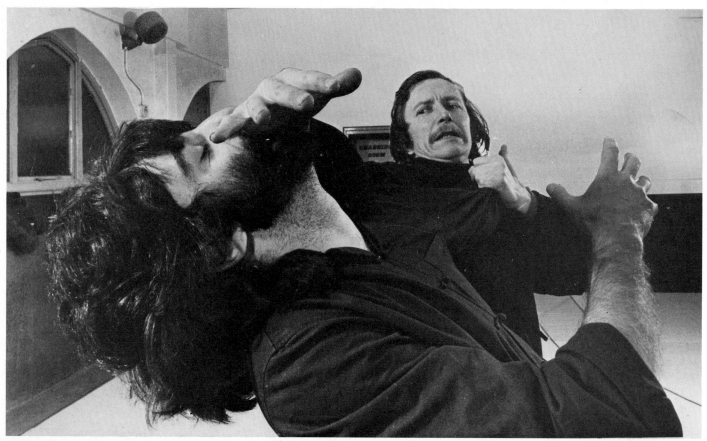

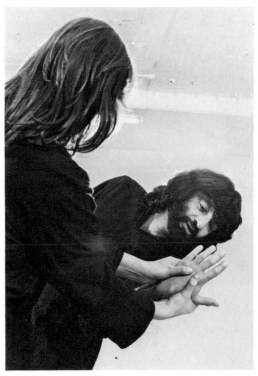

above If the girl is sufficiently quick and strong, she can bring the man to an off-balance position and give him a good kick. Such a technique of twisting the wrist and pressing on a vital point of the body requires a good deal of skill and should be regarded as a defensive measure leading to a more telling attack.

above left Crushing the fingers and applying pressure to the thumb joint just as the attacker begins to apply his hold. Once more this is a technique which should be followed by a better one.

This rough version of the judo Stomach Throw is one of a wide range of throws in ju-jutsu, and might well have been preceded by a kick in the stomach.

One of the *katsu* techniques for reviving a man after a blow in the testicles. The 'patient' lies on the floor, the legs are alternately lifted, and the soft part of the instep is tapped with the edge of the clenched fist.

Ju-jutsu throws make use of changes in height, varying from standing and leaping to throwing from the floor. This example is a type of kneeling Shoulder Wheel.

made with completely straight arms, and furthermore a very strong man cannot have his arms and wrists twisted by another man's unaided, single hand. The second example demonstrates a much more realistic situation. It is simpler and more practical to knee or to gouge the eyes, and all three possibilities are more representative of real ju-jutsu combat.

This does not mean that all less practical ju-jutsu methods should be abandoned in modern training. It does, however, serve to point out an approach which has dogged the martial arts in general, ju-jutsu being no exception. This is the stubborn and prejudiced attitude of some instructors towards the distinction between aesthetic and practical methods. Such instructors insist that all their techniques are of equal practical value when they are manifestly not. Uncritical, perhaps understandably naïve, youngsters take them at their word and can, if accosted, land in trouble by trying to carry out unsuitable techniques.

Choosing a club

How, when martial arts are so popular, does one recognize the charlatan? How can one tell if a newly opened school is authentic or not? Unlike judo, karate, and aikido, the techniques of ju-jutsu ryu are not available in book form. The modern development and organization of ju-jutsu is in fact obscure, whatever purists may say to the contrary. Such a situation is wide open to abuse. For the newcomer to ju-jutsu the best resource is a critical mind. Does a technique work in a simulated 'real' situation. If a friend grabs you, can a ju-jutsu technique you have learned help? If not, put it on one side as dubious. If none of the techniques seem to work except in an absolutely formal setting you can draw one of three conclusions: 1. the teacher is a fake; 2. he is teaching only kata movements; or 3. you are not being taught correctly.

Ju-jutsu contains a wealth of techniques and deserves a place alongside the other martial arts of the East. What it lacks today is organization and proper exposure to the general public.

Judo

Judo is a splendid physical sport and a curious hybrid art form. It attracts those who want to get fit, have fun and learn to defend themselves, and it also appeals to those with more serious ideas about life and man's efforts to control and understand himself.

There is no magic way to flick people over your head or down three armed men with a whisk of the arm or leg. Judo is a hard physical activity in which you probably use more muscles than in almost any other sport. Judo demands discipline and regular practice and, if you want to be good, dedication. Unlike sports such as golf or tennis, there are very few financial rewards for the top men, and, apart from a few teachers, *judoka* or judo exponents are all amateurs. But in compensation there is enormous satisfaction in pulling off a perfect throw and in knowing that you can look after yourself almost anywhere.

I have already suggested that people do judo to get fit or to defend themselves but there are other reasons. There is for many people something rather exciting about an oriental activity that apparently promises them power over others.

Many judoka become interested in other martial arts, and today kung fu and karate are 'trendy' in the way judo was ten or fifteen years ago. It is a good thing that people move between the martial arts or do several, but in my view judo is the best one to start with because it is more physical than the other martial arts—there is after all firm body contact most of the time in *tachiwaza* (standing judo) and *newaza* (ground or mat work)—and youngsters are more readily attracted to the variety of judo. Karate, aikido, and kung fu on the other hand have much less rough and tumble about them; they demand more control and may well be more suitable for those over the age of fifteen.

My own theory is that people who take up the martial arts are basically lonely—perhaps I should say 'alone' rather than lonely because there is a difference. Judoka are individualists—sometimes too much so—and I have rarely heard of a judoka who also excels at team games. All martial-arts people think for themselves, go their own way, and tend to have a stubborn streak! You need strong character to stick to the martial arts.

For some years now judo authorities have insisted that judo is a sport and it seems important, particularly at beginner level, that it be treated as such. Later the mental and spiritual aspects can be explored. It provides a marvellous and surprisingly safe activity for youngsters from eight or nine upwards, and more and more schools have judo classes which are invariably popular.

It is important to understand something about the history of judo but it is equally important that people interested or just curious about judo should not be bogged down in the past or become overawed by the sheer weight of tradition. The new breed of judoka do judo first and talk about it afterwards. This is how it should be and it is why I want to tell you about the *dojo*, or judo hall, and the equipment before I tell you how judo originated in Japan.

Koizumi shows two students how to pull an opponent off balance with the minimum of effort.

Beginning judo

There is only one—rather obvious—way to begin judo, by going along to a club, enrolling in a beginner's course, and sticking it out for ten or twelve lessons. It is surprising the number of people who think you can learn judo from a book. You cannot. Judo books are rather like books on music. They are useful right at the beginning to warn you what to expect and to get you into a receptive frame of mind for your training. And they are useful later on to correct errors and to stimulate you to greater efforts. But if you want to learn judo you have to have either private or group lessons from someone competent to teach.

One of the things rarely mentioned is that judo authorities normally estimate that only one out of ten people who start doing judo will continue to practise beyond the beginner stage. So don't be worried if you don't take to the sport—try aikido or karate instead—or have a look at another dojo, you may like it better.

The dojo

Judo is usually practised in a largish, airy room. On the floor of the dojo are *tatami*, or mats, which used to be made of straw covered with cloth and are now often synthetically covered. The mats usually measure about 6 feet by 3 feet, the size of Japanese room mats, and each are up to 4 inches thick. They are quite hard and resilient and they fit closely together so that there are no dangerous gaps. When you are thrown, they cushion the fall and yet still give you the sensation of hitting the floor. If the mats were too soft, your feet would sink into them like sponge, movement would be difficult, and they would clearly be useless. Equally, mats that are too hard are dangerous. I vividly recall breaking a leg at a club some years ago because its mats were excessively hard.

Older clubs often have mats covered with a large canvas sheet stretched by cords to a wooden frame. This type of mat is usually quite safe but the modern tatami that do not slip and fit neatly together are better. The very best clubs have sprung floors and the Japanese are well to the fore in this respect. Being thrown on to a mat laid on a sprung floor is really quite pleasurable and the chance of injury is of course greatly reduced.

The dojo is neither a shrine nor an ordinary room. Decoration is usually kept to a minimum, and the lighting should be good. There is usually a walking space between the edges of the mats and the walls. Most clubs have a spectator area. But the dojo is a

Geesink and Sone get to grips in the 1961 World Championships. Sone was a big man, but despite a slightly deceptive camera-angle Geesink dwarfed him.

quiet place and discipline is firm with politeness almost obtrusive. In the dojo the senior teacher is 'king'—it is quite feudal, but it works.

Judo clothes

People who practise judo wear *judogi* (special pants and jacket). The judogi is based on traditional Japanese garments and is made of immensely strong but quite soft absorbent cotton, designed to stand up to rough handling and regular washing for several years.

The pants are loose, hanging to below the knee, and are tied round the waist by an integral cord. The jacket is heavier and is also loose so as not to restrict movement, with extra-strong padded lapels and reinforced ribs where the most pressure is known to be exerted. The best judogi are made in Japan, where they manage to combine lightness and strength, an important point because the sweat pours off you during practice. The judogi jacket is held in place by a coloured belt about 2 inches wide that wraps twice around the body and ties in a reef knot at the front. The colour of the belt denotes the standard of skill achieved by the judoka and is the only mark of grade allowed. It is normal to wear underpants or *fundoshi* (Japanese loincloth) under the judogi but no vest. Ladies wear a cotton tee-shirt but no bra. There is very little difference in design between judogi for women, children, and men.

Judo is always done in bare feet, and toenails and fingernails are kept short and clean to avoid injury or disease. Jewellery, watches, rings, and hair pins, etc. are not worn because of obvious dangers, and clean judogi, hands, and feet are stressed. It is sheer bad manners to be dirty on the mat and although some clubs are more fussy than others it would be a shame to have the senior grade throw you—probably literally—out of the dojo.

If you have a dojo and a judogi—you can usually borrow the latter to begin with from the club—you have the basics. You need nothing else except an opponent and hopefully a qualified teacher. You are ready to do judo.

The origins of judo

Judo was formulated in Japan in the nineteenth century but, as with other Japanese fighting forms, it inevitably has some Chinese influence. Japan in the middle ages was a feudal land indeed, cut off from outside influences for hundreds of years. It has often been compared with medieval Europe and there was certainly something of the courtliness of King Arthur's knights about the best of the samurai. Most of them chose to serve a lord and many were totally dedicated to their masters and readily died in their service, prizing nobility and courtesy almost as much as faithfulness. But there were bands of wandering, unscrupulous samurai too and not all the lords quite lived up to Sir Lancelot's standards. Only a fool would view feudal Japan through rose-tinted spectacles. Life for most people must have been nasty, brutish, and short.

One of the samurai arts was ju-jutsu, claimed by some to have been introduced to Japan in the seventeenth century by Ching-Ping, a naturalized Chinese. It was a vicious form of self-defence taught to the samurai in private, often at secret schools run by highly skilled masters. Those who became proficient in it could throw, strangle, and break the limbs of one or several opponents. The warlike virtues of toughness were emphasized all the time but naturally in such an atmosphere injuries and deaths were not infrequent among the students. Ju-jutsu masters also taught defence with sticks and knives, and frequently a highly trained man could defeat one armed with a sword. Ju-jutsu took on a new dimension when in 1876, only twenty-three years after the first foreign traders landed on Japanese soil, the wearing of swords was forbidden. Clearly when weapons were forbidden, unarmed self-defence was bound to come into its own among the young and the energetic.

The contradictions of the Japanese character are well known. Even today it is quite normal for a businessman to leave his dictating machine, telephone, and automatic car when he returns home, slip on his kimono, accept the humble bows of his wife, and enter a world of delicacy, charm, and often stylistic simplicity. The Japanese like to have the best of both the old and the new worlds.

Dr Jigoro Kano (1860–1936), the redoubtable 'inventor' of judo, understood the contradictory nature of the Japanese well. In his youth he was a formidable fighter. He travelled throughout Japan– as other *ronin*, or masterless samurai, had done years before– studying ju-jutsu from the greatest masters. But he was an educator as well as a martial-arts expert. It was he in fact who personally influenced much of the physical-education programme of the newly structured Japanese educational system. A highly cultivated and much underestimated man, he understood that in the martial arts it is necessary to train the complete man and not just produce a thug. Thus he gradually developed judo.

Ju-do translates as the 'way or path of gentleness'–but don't be misled by that. It helps to be strong. Dr Kano took the best of the ju-jutsu techniques, developed others himself, and combined them in a complex series of training movements. He obviously eliminated moves that might kill or maim, but being a highly intelligent man he left some of the violence. In 1882 he founded the world headquarters of judo, the Kodokan, in Tokyo, and he personally trained the 'missionaries' of his art.

Before the First World War judo was intensely nationalistic and few Europeans even got the chance to see it. You can imagine the way tales were repeated and exaggerated back home in Europe by those who had seen the mysterious activity in Japan. Stories of masters who could freeze an opponent into immobility by a shout, or *kiai*, abounded, and fledgling judoka certainly did at times venture into tough areas of Tokyo and taunt the locals in order to try out their new-found skills. Not a particularly admirable phase in the development of judo but possibly a necessary one! Judo had to be effective. As in all the martial arts, it's no use complaining if your opponent doesn't put his foot or hand where you want him to or decides to hit you with a chair instead of his fist.

Kano's remarkable work was appreciated by some Japanese and slowly judo gained ground at the expense of ju-jutsu. Rules were formulated. Judo didn't become one of the most important Japanese sports overnight, but between the world wars the military

A breakfall. Note the left hand at about 45 degrees to the body. It will hit the mat before the back, thus taking much of the shock of the landing. Avoid striking the mat too close to your body or you will roll on to your arm—and it hurts. The right hand is holding the thrower's lapel, and this makes the throw less heavy. Kind throwers will actually give you a tug as you fall, an additional insurance that your left arm hits the mat before the rest of you.

hawks' realized that the discipline of judo produced tough and courageous young men and they encouraged the sport. Gradually ju-jutsu fell into disrepute, although schools still existed, but judo also had its ups and downs in popularity before being finally accepted. Nowadays the Japanese have the opportunity to do judo at school—perhaps 'to play judo' is the right phrase at that stage—and they have always made great efforts to see that their top judoka teach the young.

Recent history

Between the world wars a few Western judoka went to Japan to train but the main internationalizing impetus derived from three or four Japanese masters who came to the West. Most prominent among the pioneers were Yukio Tani, who had first arrived in 1904, and Gunji Koizumi, both of whom travelled throughout Europe, teaching and taking part in demonstrations at fairs, in factories, and anywhere they could find to show their skill. These two tiny and incredibly tough men sometimes took on twenty or thirty people one after the other. They also laid the foundations of the Budokwai club in London, on which English teachers like the great Trevor Leggett built.

One of the Westerners' problems has been that they are not just large Japanese. They are built differently and are generally less supple with longer but weaker legs. Of course there are large Japanese but Dr Kano designed his judo for the smaller man. Thus Japanese judo has to some extent to be adapted for the West although this in no way invalidates his *katas*, or series of movements designed to cover judo technique.

Since the Second World War judo in the West has gone from strength to strength. Certainly the greatest moment was the victory of the giant Dutchman, Anton Geesink, in Paris in 1961, when he became the first non-Japanese to win the World Championship. I was in the stadium at the time and will never forget the roar as he beat his third Japanese judoka to take the title. Geesink went on to prove his superiority by winning the 1964 Olympic gold medal and the World Championships in 1965. But he was 6 feet 8 inches tall, nearly 20 stone, and shaped like a pear—the ideal shape for a judo champion because an immensely low centre of gravity makes it almost impossible to be thrown!

The Geesink victory produced traumas in Japan and since then the Japanese have regained their old superiority at almost all weights by dint of their dedication, superior training methods, and sheer strength in depth. There are thousands of men in Japan of a very high standard whereas in the West each country has perhaps only two or three judoka at the highest levels. The universities are the real training ground for the top men in Japan and they can get scholarships to do judo in much the same way football scholarships are available in the USA. European universities are woefully weak because judo is still very much a minor sport there. Top contest-men the world over seem to reach their peak between the ages of about twenty-four and twenty-eight, although some are a little older and at least one Japanese judoka nearer forty than thirty has taken a world title.

There is a great nostalgia in Japan for the days of the samurai— witnessed by the popularity of samurai movies on Japanese television rather in the same way that Westerns are popular in the USA. Unfortunately, judo is sometimes regarded in the same way, as part of their cultural heritage instead of as a living, changing activity.

At its best, Japanese judo is still supreme—lithe, fluent, and less dependent on sheer strength than Western styles. But as recent contests have shown, the best Westerners are very close indeed to the Japanese best and in the heavier weights often beat them. The day a Japanese lightweight loses at Olympic level will be as significant as Geesink's great victory.

There are no accurate estimates of how many people do judo but I have heard a worldwide figure of 2,000,000 quoted, and in Britain there are certainly upwards of 40,000 men, women, and children. In France perhaps 150,000 people do judo, and in Russia and of course Japan it is extremely popular. Judo has been practised in Europe for much longer than karate and kung fu, although quite frankly these days it is the least glamorous of the martial arts—except that it is the only one so far accepted into the Olympic Games. This acceptance has naturally given it a great boost in recent years.

It really seems that the public has at last recognized judo as a sport. Today fewer people try to glamorize what has never really been a spectator sport. Faked and carefully rehearsed demonstrations can make shows more interesting, but in the long run they do a disservice to judo because onlookers expect that some of the 'magic' of one man beating half a dozen at once will rub off on them if they take up the sport.

Judo practice

When you actually start learning judo, you are taught how to bow humbly and politely to your opponent before trying to grind him into the tatami, but first it is useful to understand the grading system.

Dr Kano realized it was necessary to encourage participants and introduced three coloured belts, white, brown, and black, to denote grade standard. An improvement in grade had to be fought for and a theory examination had to be passed as well.

Britain and some other Western countries use a grading syllabus which starts at red belt, then after the first exam moves on to white belt, then yellow, orange, green, blue, brown, and black. Judoka with anything other than a black belt are called *kyu* (pupil) grades, and black-belt holders are called *dan* (teacher) grades. There is also a grading syllabus for *mon* (junior) belts, which youngsters can take before they graduate to the senior grades at the age of sixteen. The women's syllabus is similar to the male one.

A man with a blue or brown belt has usually had at least two or three years' judo experience, practising two or three times a week for 1½–2 hours each time, and he knows a wide range of throws and groundwork techniques, besides having defeated a number of men in contest. Promotion can now be achieved by winning cumulative points but it wasn't always like that, and ten years or more ago a brown belt wanting to take the big jump to black might have to

top Balance is broken to the front. Note that the lift has come from a straightening of the wrists which is quite sufficient to lift the man on to his toes and into a very weak position. If too much of a jerk is given, the opponent automatically moves a foot forward into a stronger position.

above Uki-otoshi (Floating Drop). Not a very common throw, but it admirably illustrates how the opponent's balance to the side can be completely broken by a strong downward tug created by the thrower dropping on to one knee. This photograph was not posed; the movement was completed by a breakfall because the impetus was too great for the throw to be avoided. In *randori*, or free practice, experts usually manage to throw only absolute beginners in this way.

beat as many as ten men of his own grade in succession and then demonstrate a kata.

The dan grades also have promotion categories but the colour of belt stays black up to 5th dan, when for formal occasions you could if you wished wear a red-and-white striped belt. At 10th dan— there have only been seven 10th dans, all deceased—you go back to red belt, and if anyone reaches 12th dan one day they will wear a white belt, thus completing the circle of grade colours.

In Japan the best contest-men usually are 4th or 5th dans. Above 5th dan, grading is not done on fighting ability but for devotion to judo and years of teaching. Many men in their fifties, sixties, and even seventies regularly practise judo at the Kodokan, avoiding the violent excesses of their younger compatriots and still thoroughly enjoying themselves. Some of them are practically carried to the mat but perk up like spring lambs once they get their toes on the tatami.

When you first enter a dojo, your instructor will tell you a little about the sport. Then he will almost certainly get you doing some loosening exercises. Apart from the press-ups, these are not too strenuous and are designed to ensure that tense muscles are relaxed and in good working order. All athletes know the danger of pulling a muscle because they were not loosened up before starting their sport.

Next you will be shown how to bow. Before and after every practice, each class forms a line and makes a full kneeling bow to the *sensei*, or instructor, and you will make standing bows to your opponents before each fight or training period too. Obviously you'd be foolish to shake hands with a judo man—you'd probably find yourself on your back.

Most of the terms used in judo are Japanese. This is not perverse; there are English names for the throws and locks but if you were to go to another country or even a different part of your own country you would quite likely find there were different local names for the same movement. Just as French terms are used in fencing, in judo Japanese names are known throughout the world.

The first real judo you must learn is how to breakfall. If you are thrown to the ground at 40 or 50 mph—a quite normal real speed through the air—and you cannot break your fall, you can hurt yourself. So the teacher will show you how to strike the mat with your arm at a 45-degree angle a split second before your body. The arm takes the shock, and it can sting, but in a surprisingly short time absolute beginners are doing good breakfalls. Timing is vital. If you hit the mat too soon or too late you will hurt yourself so before every practice you will see both beginners and dan grades practising their breakfalls.

The rolling breakfalls to the front and the two-handed breakfall to the rear are also done but really these are as much to engender confidence as anything else. If you can dive over half a dozen kneeling people and land on your back after completing a somersault without hurting yourself it does amazing things for your self-confidence.

It may well take three or four hours' training to do good breakfalls but most instructors start you on your first throw after

Okuri-ashi-harai (Sweeping Ankle Throw). The important thing is not to worry too much about the name—there are lots of variations— but really to lift your opponent as is admirably illustrated here.

opposite above You can't pose pictures like the one above right opposite. The man being thrown is about to perform an arc before hitting the mat somewhere out of shot on the right. This is in fact *Tsurikomi-ashi* (Propping Ankle Throw) and the thrower's left foot did the damage (*above left*). The foot was then withdrawn so the thrower did not lose his balance too.

opposite below left *O-goshi* (Major Hip Throw). This is the basic throw in which the opponent is lifted up and over the hip after his balance has been broken. Note that the thrower has got under the centre of gravity of his opponent and also that the thrower's head is twisted away to the left, giving added impetus to the circle which the man in the air is about to complete before hitting the mat.

opposite below right *Harai-goshi* (Sweeping or Floating Hip Throw). The thrower's arm goes either round the opponent's waist or, as with this slightly heavier variation, around the back of his neck.

Tai-otoshi (Body Drop Throw). The thrower should perhaps have his left leg bent more, but experienced judoka tend to do this throw from a higher, stronger position as illustrated. If you drop too low, you may be dragged backwards and strangled, particularly if you have not generated enough speed.

right   Seoi-nage (Shoulder Throw). This illustrates the more traditional arm positioning. The upward drive you must achieve comes from the bent arm with the wrist in a strong, locked position—not bent back as can easily happen. If the throw is done too slowly, your opponent will pull backwards and you will find your wrist in a weak position before you flop over backwards.

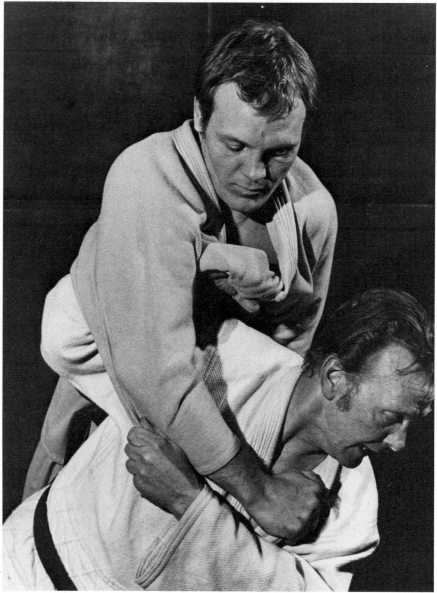

about half an hour of the first training session. Doing breakfalls is not very interesting and your arms will begin to hurt after a while. Some instructors start throwing before breakfalls to make sure their students do not get bored, but I am a little doubtful if this is really such a good idea.

The first throw to be learnt is normally *O-goshi* (the Major Hip Throw, O- always means 'major' or 'big'). This teaches the student to pick up his or her opponent, throw him over the hip, and land him cleanly on his back. It also develops balance and timing. If you do not have control of your body and are not doing the right thing at the right time, you'll fall over backwards instead of throwing your opponent.

In throwing it is vital to break your opponent's balance to the side, back, or front. You begin by holding his jacket by the lapels or by putting your left hand on his right arm and your right hand on his left lapel. Then if you push backwards and down, he must either move his feet backwards or fall over. The same applies to the sides and front. If you are pulled to the side, your balance is broken or you move to avoid the pull. The art of breaking balance may in fact require only a slight pull, not a great tug. A lift of an inch or two does not give your opponent time or inclination to move, and here is the great beauty of judo—minimum effort to achieve maximum results.

Judo is the way of least resistance—at least that's what they say—and when it is done correctly it is true and very beautiful. But it takes a long time and a lot of effort before your movements become reflexes and you really understand the simile about the power of water taking the line of least resistance and overcoming.

When the principles of the breakfall and one throw are firmly understood the instructor will progress to further throws. There are about a dozen basic throws, and every one embodies the same principles. First break balance, then move in under the centre of gravity (usually just below the navel, except for ankle sweeps), lift your opponent rapidly and smoothly, and hurl him to the mat usually on his back. Ankle sweeps are really just trips, using your foot either like a sickle to whisk away the opponent's leg or as a pivot to wheel him over to left or right. There are throws in which the foot is reaped away—*O-soto-gari*—and others in which the opponent is floated into the air—*Harai-goshi* and *Seoi-nage*. *Kata-guruma* is a very heavy throw in which you lift the man right on to your shoulders before crashing him down. Most judoka give up when they find their feet hoisted off the ground. The final main category of basic throws is the sacrifice throws, with *Tomoe-nage* (the Stomach Throw) as the most popular. It is spectacular but it has the disadvantage that, however quick you may be, you have to go down on to your own back before completing the throw. This is why sacrifice techniques have never been popular in competition.

There are two other main departments of judo: groundwork techniques (*newaza*) and striking techniques (*atemiwaza*). Dr Kano listed the striking techniques in the judo canon, but they are not permitted in contests. They are in fact virtually indistinguishable from karate moves and, although taught to high grades in Japan, are very rarely if ever seen. If you want to learn them, I suggest you take up karate and indeed many judoka do so as a secondary study.

Newaza is broken down into three sections: hold-downs, strangles, and locks—the latter almost always against arm joints.

There are a variety of hold-downs and many of them look rather similar to the amateur-wrestling holds in which you pin your struggling opponent to the mat. They don't look particularly powerful but when a determined and skilled opponent has you in such a hold you begin to realize how difficult it is to get out. Good judoka can move from hold to hold to counter your movements.

One of the things you soon learn is how to give in or surrender. When you have decided to submit because pain, fear of a broken limb or maybe even a strangle hold has you on the verge of unconsciousness, you tap your opponent three or four times quickly on any part of his body or, if your arms are trapped, stamp your feet or even cry out that you give in. Any way will do to show clearly that you have had enough. Your opponent will release his lock or hold immediately.

Locks are put on in groundwork or sometimes in a standing position, although this is quite unusual. Basically, all you do is

top Tomoe-nage (Stomach Throw). Please avoid putting your foot in a place your opponent won't like. Make sure that the main impetus for this throw comes from the arms, which drag your man very quickly down before the foot acts as a pivot dug into the stomach.

above Uchi-mata (Inner Thigh Throw). Not an easy throw, but it is one of the most popular in contest and it demands total commitment on the part of the thrower. The same applies as for Tomoe-nage!

right and opposite left *Kata-guruma* (Shoulder Wheel). Most people give up when they are lifted off the ground in this position reminiscent of professional wrestling. The left-hand picture opposite shows you just what happens if you don't give in. Believe me, it's a heavy throw which usually knocks the wind right out of you.

catch hold of an opponent's limb in such a way that he cannot escape. Locks can certainly hurt and only the silly fail to tap. Kidney squeezes are not allowed because of the danger, and one rarely sees leg locks because the legs are so strong. Combinations of holds and locks are quite common and you may soon be working them out for yourself as you roll around the mat trying to 'tie up' your opponent.

You'll never be in much doubt about whether you're being strangled! The pressure comes against the throat or against the carotid arteries, which run on either side of the neck and carry blood to the brain. They are protected by muscles which can be moved aside by a quick forward jerk and unconsciousness can result in about 20 seconds if the strangle is correctly applied from front or rear. This can be dangerous but it is to the credit of all judoka that no one to my knowledge has ever died in the West as the direct result of a strangle. Indeed only four or five judoka have ever died doing judo and all had heart-attacks and probably should not have been practising at all.

In a contest the referee usually allows the rough and tumble of groundwork to continue until one of the fighters stands up, they both roll off the mat, or it is clear that neither of them can get a hold-down. If one of the fighters escapes from a hold in less than 30 seconds, he avoids losing the contest. And that leads me on to explaining how judo contests are won.

top *Ura-nage* (Rear Throw). You won't be too popular if you land this one on your friends as performed here but it shows you just what can happen to an attacker.

centre *Kesa-gatame* (Scarf Holding), the basic groundwork hold so called for obvious reasons. The legs of the holder are spread wide and braced to give him a strong triangular position. If lifted, the arm around the neck tends to lock it in the same way as in *Kataha-jime* (page 98).

above *Kami-shiho-gatame* (Upper Four-quarters Hold-down). Like most of the hold-downs, it is much more difficult to escape than you think. Skilled men move their weight to counter frantic escape movements.

right A standing arm-lock. The pressure against the elbow is produced by a turning movement that also forces the opponent on to his face. Extra leverage can be applied by the thrower joining his hands together to produce a vicious lock as here.

below Juji-gatame (Straight Arm-lock sometimes rather confusingly called Cross Arm-lock). In this highly effective lock, pain is produced against the elbow joint, which will break if pressure is continued. Give in before that happens!

right Ude-garami (Figure-Four Arm-lock). It looks rather a tangle but a little detective work will prove that the man underneath has a painful elbow joint.

opposite Ude-gatame (Arm Crush Lock). This can be applied from almost any position. Similar locks are often favoured by policemen apprehending villains.

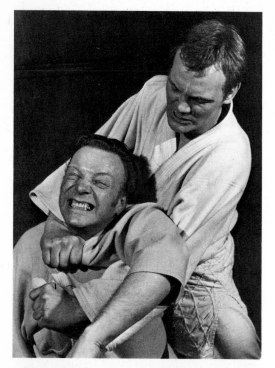

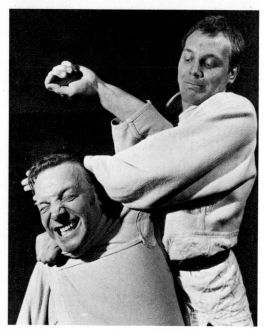

top Okuri-eri-jime (Sliding Collar Neck-lock). The grimace is not put on for the camera. When you are neck-locked, it is almost impossible to remain impassive. The eyes close and you fight for breath.

above Kataha-jime (Single Wing Choke). Both the opponent's arm and neck are trapped by this movement. Its effectiveness derives from the fact that the head is pushed forward and this tends to immobilize the neck.

Victory and loss

Victory comes in several ways. A clean throw with your opponent landing with a thump on his back gets you an *ippon*, or full point, and that's the end of the contest. A hold-down for 30 seconds also wins a full point, and a submission because of the pain of a lock or strangle is another way of winning.

The referee can call a halt if one contestant strikes or gouges his opponent. Judo referees are very keen on politeness and crack down hard on viciousness but it would be silly to pretend that, particularly at international level, there is not great emphasis on winning. The Japanese are incredibly victory conscious and it is said that a Japanese judoka who loses a major contest will never fight for his country again. But this is a far cry from the average dojo practice, when no one tries to hurt anyone else and when the thug quickly finds the instructor bouncing *him*. Judoka don't like bullies.

Half points are awarded for throws that just miss and hold-downs broken after 25 seconds. Good attempts in contest win fractions of a point. I should explain that if both competitors fall over, then they can go directly into groundwork without pause.

Some men are known to be newaza experts just as some are famous for particular left-hand or right-hand throws or combinations of throws. All moves are done to both sides. It is part of advanced judo technique to pretend to go for a hip throw to the right and then throw with the leg to the left or vice-versa. Whole series of combination techniques have been worked out and, as in boxing, top contest-men study their opponents' favourite moves and try to assess weaknesses. It is illegal deliberately to drag your opponent into groundwork but all sorts of ruses and ploys are used by the ruthless who fancy their ability on the mat.

Weight categories

For some years now weight categories have been accepted in judo. In the old days small men fought large, and frankly usually lost. A skilful small man will always beat an untrained or half-trained big man, but if the small and large man have roughly equal skills, as at international level, the large man will always swamp the lighter opponent.

After a lot of debate and shaking of heads from those who predicted that weight categories heralded the end of judo, they were accepted and have proved sensible and practical ever since. The categories are as follows: lightweight, light-middleweight, middleweight, light-heavyweight, and heavyweight. There are no weight categories at gradings, and at contests there is usually also an open category, in which any one can compete.

Randori

If you train twice a week, after only three or four weeks you will probably be introduced to strangles and groundwork moves. You'll have the pleasure of choking your colleagues – carefully I trust.

After six or seven weeks you may well get the chance to do *randori* or free practice. At first it is a bit frightening with both of you trying to throw or hold the other down rather than co-operating with each other. However, if reasonable precautions are taken, it is enormous fun and a real thrill when you bring off a throw. Beginners are usually encouraged to ask the higher grades for a practice and you'll get plenty of breakfall training as they land you more or less at will with varying degrees of gentleness all over the mat with a whole variety of throws.

About half your time on the mat will be taken up with randori and it sharpens your reactions no end. Aikido and karate both have competitive formats for the higher grades, but judo is the only one of the martial arts that offers so much randori to relative beginners. It is hard and sweaty work but it is the basis of judo today.

The rest of your time in the dojo will be taken up with demonstrations of throws, locks, and escape movements, with exercises and breakfalls (ukemi), with uchikomi (repetitive movements to perfect a throw without actually throwing), and with actual completed throws against an either helpful or resisting opponent. The aim of uchikomi is, of course, to learn the technique and to be able to use it when the opportunity occurs. Your opponent is not always going to be helping you in contest or real life, but initially in practice it is important to do slow moves that break balance and take your partner to the point of completing the throw. You might do a hundred repetitions of each movement. In Japan some masters make their students do a thousand or more uchikomi repetitions in a night. Whatever happens, there will be relatively little chat. Most judoka get on with judo and do their chattering over a drink afterwards.

At the end of practice some sensei make their students kneel, close their eyes, and stay still for a few minutes. This can be enormously relaxing and is a form of meditation. Then comes the bow, sometimes made several times, depending on who is present.

When the session is over, take a well-earned shower or bath. You'll need it and tired and aching muscles certainly appreciate it. You will be very stiff indeed at first because judo's unaccustomed movements bring muscles into action you didn't even know you had. Do not avoid the bath or shower, and, if the club is too small to have such facilities, have one at home as soon as you possibly can. If you can afford a massage—and it is available—it is well worthwhile. I recall that I could hardly move my neck and shoulders for a week after first being introduced to the strangles, and my wrists felt so weak I had trouble lifting my pen. But if you stick it out the stiffness goes, and you begin to tingle with health and vitality. Your body enjoys being 'stretched'.

As you progress, make time to watch top judoka in action. Eventually you will take gradings, and senior instructors will test your skill and watch you compete. Gradings are invariably nervous times and are in fact as much a test of your mental approach and confidence as anything else. My first grading passed in a sort of dream and incidentally, to my surprise, I did rather well.

Competition judo is, as I have indicated, very tough these days. Top judoka train fanatically hard with weights, running, and exercises. They almost certainly practise at least once a day and give the distinct impression of being made of iron. But you're not going to fight these people on equal terms for at least five or six years unless you are completely exceptional.

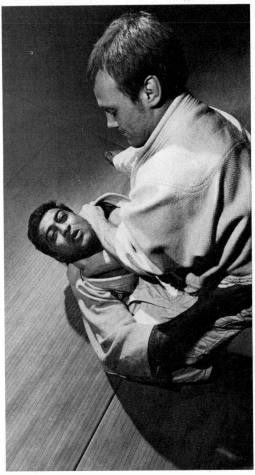

top The muscles protecting the carotid arteries are moved forward by a slight movement of the hands, and pressure for a few seconds will produce unconsciousness with no pain. Neck-locks and strangles are either done against the carotids or the jugular.

above *Kataju-jime* (Half-Cross Strangle). This is a popular attack against the carotid arteries. If the attacker leans over his opponent's head, even more pressure is applied.

The effort involved in groundwork is well illustrated by this up-to-date version of *Hadaka-jime* (Naked Strangle), so named because it can be done equally effectively against an opponent whether or not he is wearing clothes.

A conscientious person who trains hard three times a week and does the occasional weekend or longer course can expect to reach 1st dan in three or four years, although it has been done in six months. But many judoka settle for brown or blue belts. Grades in Western countries are, incidentally, much harder to get than Japanese grades. In fact East Germany and Britain are probably the toughest nations from a promotion point of view, even though it is now far easier than it used to be. A few years ago I saw a 1st dan beat ten other 1st dans and eight brown belts in succession and still be refused his 2nd dan because the examiners did not like his style. Things have changed today and incidentally that man went on to become one of Britain's finest ever judoka.

The katas

After you have been doing judo for a while you will hear about and eventually be introduced to the *katas*. These are stylized throws or movements always repeated in the same way by two people and designed to cover virtually the whole range of judo.

Dr Kano himself largely originated the katas and insisted on his students studying what he considered to be the real basis of judo. Today most of us see randori in that light, but, although young judoka almost invariably prefer free-style practice, it is very impressive to see a kata performed by two people who seem almost to be reading each other's minds to reach synchronized perfection.

The katas have been out of favour in the West recently because many people consider them rather dull, particularly as they are usually done very slowly. But some, mostly higher grade, judoka find great satisfaction in mastering several katas. They are probably due to be 'rediscovered' soon and variations on the traditional seven, done at speed, can be more interesting to do.

There are literally thousands of katas but these seven seem to have been recognized as basic and they contain meticulous, carefully chosen, and classified moves which have over the years been refined to show pure judo. The most basic of all katas is called *Nage-no-kata* (the Kata of Throws) and it consists of fifteen throws broken down into hand techniques, hip throws, leg and foot throws, and sacrifice throws. Another of the basic seven katas even includes defensive moves against knife and sword attacks — but such moves are rarely seen today. You don't come across a lot of people wandering the streets these days wearing *katana*, or Japanese swords. But there are always judoka keen on tradition who would probably like to have been born in samurai times.

It does not do, however, to underestimate the katas; they are very demanding. You need controlled strength and discipline to perform the movement either very slowly as in tai chi or at a fast fluent pace. You also need to be willing to take great pains to perfect the moves.

Women and judo

A surprisingly large number of women do judo and some of them are rather good. I say surprisingly because I am chauvinistic enough to believe that aikido is probably more suitable for the fair sex. My wife, who was born in Japan, agrees with me but a lot of Western lady judoka disagree strongly. The fact does, however, remain that judo is a marvellous exercise for women and, with a few exceptions, lady judoka remain very feminine. They can do practically all the moves done by the men but I find groundwork rather ugly at times when they perform it. Katas, on the other hand, can be most graceful when performed by women.

Children and judo

Judo is really suitable for the children. They love it. To watch the small children at the Kodokan in Japan is a joy as they bustle about, throw each other with abandon, and race back for more. They hardly ever seem to get hurt and roll about with shrieks of delight which their teachers find difficult to suppress. Little girls seem to have just as much fun and all the international judo associations have recognized the importance of school judo.

Eight or nine may be the optimum age to start judo, but it is really impossible to generalize. Five- and six-year-olds have been known to enjoy it immensely, and at least two of Britain's best judoka did not start until well past their twenty-first birthdays.

Judo for the older man

I hardly need to mention that as you get older reactions slow down and it is easy to get 'lazy' about taking physical exercise. This is a pity. Far more die of heart-attacks from not taking exercise than from taking too much. Judo is just as good a sport for the forty- or fifty-year-old as for the twenty-year-old.

The only difference is that you take it easier. Instead of having a hard contest with the young man who has just got his 2nd dan, you do a light randori, perfect that technique you never quite had time to master years before, or spread your knowledge and experience by helping beginners. In the West we could certainly make more use of the experience of the older judoka. There are, however, some most formidable men still practising in their sixties and as you get older you can often make up for strength with guile and for drive with sheer sneakiness.

Improving your judo

When you are practising judo, you cannot relax for a moment. Always there is movement and resistance, push and pull. After years of training, the throws do, however, become more and more automatic and instinctive. When you first perform a throw, find your opponent flat on his back, and are not really sure how or with what technique you actually threw him, then you are on your way to doing real judo. There was no resistance because you got it right. Your speed, skill, timing, and balance all combined for a split-second and your man was literally eliminated. It is a wonderful moment and can make years of effort seem suddenly all worthwhile. And as you ponder how to do it again, you soon begin to understand that such a throw cannot be willed—just performed.

Zen and judo

So far I have deliberately considered judo only as a sport because this is the way the majority of judoka see it—and it is right that it

top Blue belt Anne Waterman throws a fellow police cadet with *Tomoe-nage* at a careers' exhibition at London's Olympia in 1971.

above Future judo champions fight it out at London's Crystal Palace. The youngsters take things very seriously and there is an ever-increasing number of immensely popular junior and youth events.

The powerful Dave Starbrook holds compatriot Roy Inman in *Kesa-gatame* during the British Championships. See how Starbrook's left hand has locked behind his opponent's neck, pushing Inman's head on to his chest. This reduces the amount of leverage Inman can manage during escape bids.

should be so. But there is rather more to judo. Dr Kano knew it and a relatively small proportion of judoka in each generation since then have known it too.

Wherever you dip below the surface of judo—and indeed all the martial arts—you come across Zen. So first let us try to define the term. Zen translates as 'meditation' in Japanese. And meditation is one method of achieving self-realization. There are others but this particular one was developed first in China and then Japan and it was based on what the Buddha, who lived in India, had taught. Its most important precept is the necessity of meditation.

Unfortunately, there is a great deal of rubbish talked about meditation, which is not some weird oriental trick but a perfectly sensible method of first concentrating and then clearing the mind to bring it under the control of the will. By continuous practice of meditation—which I might add is very hard work indeed—we eventually break through our self-created ignorance and experience enlightenment, or *satori* or *samadhi* as the Indians call it.

Do not be worried by all the strange and contradictory things you may have read about Zen masters and the black-robed, shaven-headed, cross-legged monks. All they are doing is accepting a discipline to achieve satori more quickly and efficiently. It is not my purpose to go into the methods used by Zen teachers but so much of Zen culture has been drawn into judo and other martial arts—even the jargon we use in many cases comes from Zen—that you should have some acquaintance with it. Some judoka say that all the best things in judo are drawn from Zen—such as the tradition that the high grades always help the low grades in randori or uchikomi and that judo should naturally lead to meditation.

Mentally the Zen-judo man will not make excuses and will achieve what he sets out to do. Spiritually he will contribute to life with zestful energy. There is no doubt in my mind that the best judoka—and not necessarily the most successful or the toughest—understand something of Zen and practise meditation even if they don't actually realize they are doing so. They tend to be people who have nothing to prove. They know their own capabilities, are unworried by defeat, and take victory in their stride.

This type of person also seems to be unimpressed and often completely uninterested in getting a higher coloured belt or grade. I have met green and blue belts who should have been 2nd or even 3rd dans but who never bothered to enter gradings. I do not recommend this approach because it misleads those who fight with them and in some cases could be counted as 'pride in reverse', but these people exist.

There is a story in Japan, probably apocryphal, about a judoka who emerged from the mountains after being missing for ten years, arrived at the Kodokan, and completely demolished everybody in the place with a truly devastating hip throw. As he prepared to leave, he was asked where he was going and replied that he was off back to the mountains—to study foot throws.

I should make it clear that meditation is only a part of Zen training. Living in accord with the high principles set down by the Buddha, using your intelligence and courage as well as having a fair helping of patience and forbearance also matter. Experienced judoka rarely if ever lose their tempers however provoked—calmness is something that gradually becomes part of your make-up no matter how volatile you were by temperament when you started judo. I am sure you have heard stories of how young thugs started judo and were transformed into upright citizens. I suspect that such transformations are exaggerated but they certainly have sometimes happened.

Pentchev of Bulgaria throws Wooley of the USA with a massive *Ippon Seoi-nage* (Shoulder Throw). Note how for a fraction of a second—before he turns completely—Pentchev's driving right-hand is touching the mat.

Judo injuries

I sincerely hope this little section is not going to put anyone off judo. For an active, explosive sport there are very few injuries indeed and those that do happen are usually more inconvenient than serious. Nevertheless, a few words of warning may well save you pain and trouble.

The principal accident areas are knees and elbows. Westerners have weaker knees than the Japanese because we spend our leisure sitting in chairs instead of sitting on the floor. If you intend to do judo seriously, you would be well advised to do knee bends and exercises to firm up your thigh muscles. A few yoga exercises practised sensibly will also do a great deal for you if performed daily.

The first few times you do judo, as I have said, you will be very stiff and you will—quite soon—experience what we call 'mat burn'. This is caused by your relatively tender skin being dragged across the mat at speed, thus forming a small blister. The blister always seems to pop and you have a nasty red patch that may not bleed but which hurts. Finger joints, toes, and elbows seem to be the most vulnerable, and until the skin hardens up there is little you can do except cover the offending area with a bandage or a big plaster (small ones usually come off because of sweat). Mat burns need not stop you doing judo but do use antiseptic ointment to protect, and possibly surgical spirit to toughen, the areas affected. After a few

Brian Jacks attacks with left *Uchi-mata*. Even though his left arm is in a weak position, the power of his entry—he's literally diving at the mat himself—ensures that the throw is an effective one.

below Ninomiya throws Glahn of West Germany in 8 seconds with *O-soto-gari*. You can almost feel the total commitment of this throw—there was no holding back here.

months your skin hardens and you never seem to be troubled in this way again.

Most injuries are caused by twists against the joint. A good osteopath quickly seen can do wonders. Few doctors appear to know much about this sort of injury or frankly seem very interested, but qualified osteopaths get a very good general training so do not just see them about bone troubles. If you do get a more serious injury, do not be tempted back on to the mat too soon. When you are able to, do light exercises at home, and when you do return, stick to uchikomi in short sessions for a while.

Bruised shins and calves are caused by attempted foot throws that finish up as kicks. My advice – do not kick others as you would wish them to avoid kicking you! There are also certain throws and locks that seem to have a high injury-rating and in my experience *Tai-otoshi* (the Body Drop Throw) is the worst offender. Although it is necessary to learn it, you would do well to use it sparingly in randori and contest.

There is a whole department of the martial arts called *katsu* (resuscitation techniques) that, like the katas, is probably due for rediscovery. Today very few high grades have much expertise in katsu. I have warned that strangles can be dangerous – part of katsu includes techniques for reviving the injured. Sometimes one can receive a kick or chop by accident and katsu skilfully applied can prevent pain and reduce recovery time.

Tips

When you go to a dojo, take with you a pair of slippers for getting from the changing room to the mat. Special Japanese slippers are popular. And do not forget a towel and possibly soap.

When it comes to buying a judogi, buy a good Japanese one if you possibly can. If you stick to judo it will repay the initial difference in outlay many times over, and, if you do not, you can probably sell it secondhand without difficulty. Wash your judogi often; it keeps it in good condition and you will certainly be more popular.

If you learn at a small club, there will of necessity probably be few facilities and it is quite likely that you will have to lay and lift the mats yourselves for each practice session. Do not try to avoid this chore. It is my experience that the most willing 'mat lifters' make the best judoka in the long run. Regard it as part of your training.

Try to see at least one big contest, although you may be bored by much of the judo for the best techniques always come in the early contests not the finals, when the competitors are so evenly matched. Visit a few clubs. Instructors' methods differ and so do standards. Do not be frightened to ask questions but obey instructions from the high grades. And if you should be doubtful about an instructor's qualifications, check him out with his association.

Finally, enjoy your judo. Do not make it a chore. If you should have to stop for a few weeks for any reason, the decision to return to the mat is always hard. Excuses abound. But once you get back you will be seized by the old enthusiasm.

Aikido

The roots of modern aikido lie in aiki-jujutsu and ninth-century Japan. It was a time of violence, with many clans laying claim and counter-claim to the territory and titles of others, and *bujutsu*, or classical methods of martial training, had begun to play a prominent part in the creation of the Japanese warrior class. Unarmed defensive skills were taught alongside the use of weapons, and the 'weapon' was as likely to be a tool or farming implement as some more traditional piece of military equipment. The warrior had to be skilled in defending himself against every possible method of attack and in all circumstances. Aiki-jujutsu was only one of a number of different fighting systems and schools. All of them encouraged a strict code of discipline and required their members to maintain complete secrecy as regards training methods and techniques, while laying emphasis on acquiring split-second reactions and flexibility.

Aiki-jujutsu is said to have been devised by an accomplished warrior, Prince Teijun, a son of Emperor Seiwa. Teijun's method was based on empty-handed sword strokes which were aimed at various openings in the opponent's armour. One of Teijun's sons, called Tsunemoto, extended the range of techniques, laying emphasis on the importance of *ma-ai* (judging the distance between yourself and your opponent). This ability was essential to all warriors, as they had to be prepared to meet weapons of varying length. With occasional additions and alterations the system was passed on to succeeding generations of the Minamoto clan until the twelfth century and Shinra Saburo Yoshimitsu.

Yoshimitsu was an outstanding general and a brilliant tactician, knowledgeable in many martial arts. He was also a man of vast medical knowledge, gleaned from his interest in human anatomy, which it is said he obtained first hand by dissecting the bodies of dead warriors. He improved and extended aiki-jujutsu by applying existing techniques in a more skilful way, thus enabling him to gain and keep greater control over his opponent. He realized that a warrior's hands and wrists, uncovered and unprotected as they were, could be especially vulnerable, and he therefore initiated techniques that could be applied against these points. He called the system Daito-ryu Aiki-Jujutsu, after his estate, Daito.

Yoshimitsu's son Yoshikiyo, also an accomplished warrior, enlarged the number of techniques still further by adding systems that could be used by unarmed warriors against the long and short sword. In the training he would have his unarmed warriors face skilled swordsmen. For hours they would train the co-ordination of eye and body movement necessary to avoid the swordsman's attacking strokes. Eventually this brought about an instinctive awareness of counter-attack opportunity. Yoshikiyo also instigated similar training against the halberd and the *naginata*, which is a form of slashing spear. Because of the length of these weapons and their use in large sweeping attacks at the head or legs, timing had to be perfect, and the warrior had to move in very fast to attack at the point of grasp.

It was also during Yoshikiyo's lifetime that the family's name was changed to Takeda, this being his place of residence. As time passed, the system developed still further but it continued to be kept secret within the family and among a small number of trusted retainers. In the second half of the fourteenth century the family moved again. This time to Aizu, in the northern island of Japan. It was here that another name, Aizu-todome, was attached to the system.

With the introduction of gunpowder and firearms (*hojutsu*), the ancient skills of the warrior began to decline. Although many considered the firearm a cowardly weapon, they could not ignore the fact that a warrior so armed could keep well away from any swordsman while firing a fatal shot. Consequently many of the old martial training-methods were discarded and warriors were trained in firearm drill.

In the late nineteenth century, with Japan emerging from isolation, Sogaku Takeda, the thirty-second in line of the Takeda family, decided on a revival of the family's system. He travelled Japan, teaching selected members of the nobility, and finally settled down and opened a school at Hokkaido in the province of Abashiri. It flourished, and members of the armed services studied there. His son, Tokimune Takeda, continued the school, which he named the 'Daitokan', a name it retains to the present day.

It was to this school that a man called Morei Uyeshiba went to study. Under Sogaku Takeda, Uyeshiba, already a very knowledgeable master of the martial arts, helped in the development and expansion of the school's curriculum, by introducing the best from other martial arts, as well as a number of his own ideas. He quickly became one of Sogaku Takeda's outstanding pupils.

Uyeshiba was born in Wakayama prefecture, Japan. When quite young, he had become interested in physical fitness, and through this a devotee of the martial arts. He studied at numerous schools throughout the country, including of course Takeda's school at Hokkaido, staying at each until he became proficient in its particular system. He seemed to have an insatiable desire to learn as many methods as possible, spending all his money to study under the finest masters in the land. He continued his training in the martial arts during his army service in the Russo-Japanese war, taking a delight in demonstrating his prowess. After the war, he tried his hand at numerous jobs, but was still obsessed with improving his martial skill, wishing to become, at least in his own mind, invincible.

Yoroi-kumiuchi, or grappling in armour, became a necessary system of fighting for all warriors in the event of the loss or abandonment of their weapons. But such grappling should not be mistaken for unarmed combat because warriors would at times resort to this system even when armed. Print by Yoshikazu. Victoria and Albert Museum, London.

Morei Uyeshiba, founder of the modern discipline aikido, through which he hoped everyone would learn the spirit of universal love.

It was at this stage that he came into close contact with Buddhist monks and, listening to their philosophy, began to suspect that the martial arts were more than just a means of defeating another person or of knocking him down. Typically, he decided to pursue this philosophical aspect further by entering a temple and spending many hours each day in solitude and meditation. It is said that the true meaning of the martial arts came to him as he was bathing at a well. He realized that they should not be concerned solely with force but were a way to develop a unity of mind and body. Aiki-jujutsu, as it was being practised, did not propound this philosophy so he decided to create a new art which would fulfil the principle of spiritual and physical harmony that he envisaged. He named this art 'aikido'. As with other modern martial disciplines, the suffix *jutsu* meaning 'fighting art' was dropped and *do* meaning 'the way'—indicating a gentler form—was substituted.

The word 'aikido' breaks down syllable by syllable as follows:
'ai'—harmony, to unite, co-ordinate, bring into
'ki'—spirit, energy, mental power, inner strength
'do'—the way, the method, system, even how or why
It has been interpreted in many ways, but all imply 'way of harmony'.

Uyeshiba laid down the principle of non-resistance, the non-violent way of defending one's self. By co-ordinating one's movement with another's, one could learn to bring the opponent's strength into one's own sphere, thereby neutralizing the attack. No matter what form it took, Uyeshiba would only do enough to bring the attacker under control, with as little physical harm as possible. Once he had developed his system, he began teaching selected pupils—some from noble families, others from the armed forces—continuing his instruction until the beginning of the Second World War. During the war he returned to the countryside, where he lived very simply on the land. He took with him a few students and would occasionally receive visits from others. All of them he instructed in aikido, but lessons contained more mental exercises than physical ones, part of each day being spent in meditation and mental training.

The war and the events that followed troubled him greatly. How could it be otherwise? Here was a man who realized the futility of conflict and who preached the principle of non-resistance. He saw many of his own countrymen turn away from spiritual matters and interest themselves primarily in material things. Eventually he decided that perhaps through the medium of aikido with its principles of spiritual and physical unity he could encourage the rebirth of the spirit. He contacted some of his former students and told them of his intention to make aikido, the way of harmony and truth, known throughout the world. He worked diligently and so did his students. Then he selected the best and they were sent abroad to teach aikido—some to the United States, others to Europe.

One of the most outstanding of these 'ambassadors' was Koichi Tohei, at the time 8th Dan Aikido. Tohei had studied under Uyeshiba for many years, both before and after the war. He was also a devotee of Zen and an ardent student of breath control, which he claimed helped him in his aikido training. Uyeshiba sent him to teach aikido in Hawaii, where he stayed for a year during 1953–4. He subsequently returned for short periods and in all spent seven years in America. Tohei's pleasant personality and his undoubted skill did much to promote aikido in the States, and he also encouraged many Americans to go to Japan and train under Uyeshiba. He taught the Hawaiian police and special units of the American armed forces. On his final return to Japan he became chief instructor at the aikido *hombu*, or headquarters in Tokyo. The current director of the hombu dojo is Uyeshiba's son, Kisshomaru Uyeshiba, who strictly adheres to the principles his father laid down. He took up his appointment sometime before his father's death in the 1960s, dedicating himself to the furtherance of his father's ideals.

Another who has been responsible for the promotion of Uyeshiba Aikido in the United States is Yoshimitsu Yamada. Yamada devised his own system, which slightly differs from that taught at the hombu in Tokyo. His examination syllabus also requires a longer period of study for each of the *kyu*, or student, grades. However, in general he still adheres closely to the principles of the Uyeshiba school.

Tadashi Abe 6th Dan travelled to Europe to teach aikido. He spent many years training students and followed the hombu pattern of instruction and promotion. Like Tohei, Abe encouraged many of his pupils to go to Japan and study, so that on their return they could better assist him in his efforts to promote aikido. There is now a very large following throughout Europe with the number of students increasing daily. Many other Japanese instructors followed Abe, and although their interpretation of their master's aikido varies they still continue to promote interest and enthusiasm for the Uyeshiba school.

Other pupils of Uyeshiba branched out with different interpretations, whilst still retaining the basic principles and techniques. One very famous pupil of Uyeshiba is Gozo Shioda 9th Dan Aikido, director of the Aikido Yoshinkan. The slightly built Shioda was born in Tokyo in 1915. After many years of study under Uyeshiba, his demonstrations impressed a number of businessmen, who invited him to become the chief instructor at the Yoshinkan school of aikido. His contribution to the growth of aikido has been extensive. He organized a system whereby his students were trained to become teachers and were sent out to various countries to demonstrate the effectiveness of the Yoshinkan system. The success of these missions brought a large influx of foreign students into Japan to study at the Yoshinkai Institute. Shioda is also head instructor to the Tokyo Metropolitan Police Department and at various universities including Takushoku University, from which he graduated. He lays emphasis on fast dynamic action, incorporating large circular movements, and advocates the non-strength approach to aikido.

Because of the close association with the Tokyo police, Shioda advocates the self-defence aspects of aikido more than some other masters. He is recognized as one of the greatest practitioners of aikido in Japan and is regarded with deep respect by other aikido masters. His methods of instruction differ from other schools, but

Professor Kenji Tomiki, who in 1930 studied aikido under Professor Uyeshiba. Now in his seventies he is still teaching aikido at Waseda University.

opposite below left Kokyu-nage (Breath Throw). Known as a 'breath power' throw, it is used to teach the blending of one's *ki*, or inner energy, with that of an opponent.

opposite above right Kote-gaeshi (Outside Turn). Two hands are used here to bring about the outward twisting of the wrist. In the final stage of this technique the wrist is pushed towards the attacker's shoulder.

opposite centre right Sumi-otoshi (Side Drop). The sixteenth movement of the Randori no Kata being used as a continuation technique after an attempt to avoid the initial entry for *Mae-otoshi*. A key factor is to ensure that the arm action is similar to that used when performing a downward sword cut.

opposite below right Koshi-nage (Hip Projection). Having been grasped on both wrists from behind, the defender circles the arms, steps backwards and sideways, and throws the attacker forward over the hip as though to strike down with a sword.

the great regard he has for the principles of Morei Uyeshiba is still evident.

Another important name in aikido is that of Kenji Tomiki, Professor of Physical Education at Waseda University and respected member of the Kodokan. Tomiki studied judo under its founder, Dr Kano, and when a 5th Dan Judo was asked by Kano to learn aikido under Morei Uyeshiba. This he did, and, after extensive study, returned to Kano and formulated a system of self-defence known as the *Goshin-jitsu-kata*.

Being a professor of physical education, Tomiki had delved deeply into the possibilities of aikido as a form of physical exercise, whilst still respecting Uyeshiba's thoughts on the spiritual side of aikido. Already a recognized authority on Japanese bujutsu and an accomplished expert in many martial arts, he decided to devise a system of instruction based on the principles of physical education.

Until this time no real system of instruction existed. Tomiki based his syllabus on the fundamental principle of movement, formulated into a series of exercises and a basic *kata*, or number of techniques in sequence, from which many variations stem. After some years, he decided to extend his system, which originally consisted of fifteen basic techniques. He added two more techniques to the kata and, slightly altering some of the others, he called it the Randori no Kata—or techniques suitable for *randori* or free-style situations.

He then developed a progressive method whereby these techniques could be incorporated into a free-style situation. Initially the student was trained to defend himself against a fast-moving attacker who could use any method of unarmed attack but who would not resist technique. Having attained a certain proficiency, the student then faced more than one attacker. Next weapons—the knife, sword, or *bo* (staff)—were introduced to increase the stress factor. Later Tomiki devised a series of competitive forms which tested the student's ability to defend himself in free-style situations, thereby introducing a 'sport' element into aikido.

He also further extended the formal side of aikido by adapting a number of *koryus* or ancient forms, techniques against various weapons used in other martial-art disciplines and in classical bujutsu. Although these forms are historical in content, they do offer the student a deeper understanding of aikido and a wider variety of possible techniques. Professor Tomiki is still Professor of Physical Education at Waseda University, and, though in his seventies, he can still be seen instructing students in his system.

Many of Tomiki's students have travelled and taught abroad. The first of these was Senta Yamada, who went to Britain. He studied under both Uyeshiba and Tomiki, proving himself an apt pupil by attaining his 6th Dan. He was also a 6th Dan Judo and 2nd Dan Kendo. Although slight of build, he had considerable power combined with gracefulness of movement. He quickly mastered English and, giving demonstrations throughout the country, soon had an ardent group of followers. Other Tomiki instructors followed, such as Hiroaki Kogure 5th Dan, Tsunemitsu Naito 5th Dan, Takeshi Inoue 5th Dan, and Tetsu Ehara 5th Dan. Each contributed to the growth and progress of Tomiki Aikido throughout Great Britain. Kondo 5th Dan, based in his Geneva headquarters, has been responsible for the spreading of Tomiki Aikido throughout the rest of Europe, ably assisted at times by Ehara; and Hiroaki Kogure was the one who introduced Tomiki Aikido to the USA.

The principles of aikido

Aikido may not have the dramatic impact of some other martial arts, but it has tremendous value for its students. First, there is the development of rhythmic movement and physical fitness, both integral parts of self-defence training. Second, it encourages discipline and a non-violent attitude towards the opponent. Third, it teaches the effective twisting, bending, and stretching of the joints and limbs, thus enabling them to become supple and strong, and freeing them from harmful adhesions. Lastly, it increases the student's awareness of posture and good body-alignment and improves reactions, perception, and co-ordination. The student learns to use the opponent's force, bringing that force into his own circle and thus neutralizing the aggressive action and bringing the attacker under control.

The execution of aikido requires considerable skill: the right technique must be properly executed at the correct time with sufficient force to attain one's objective. This implies, of course,

Mae-otoshi (Arm Push). The fifteenth movement of the Randori no Kata, in which the projection is brought about by the defender applying pressure against the attacker's upper arm and driving his body forward. This technique has numerous variations and is used to neutralize many attacking situations.

that if necessary the total amount of force available will be used. When two evenly matched men are practising in a free-style situation, the one who can bring his total power potential to bear in the execution of his technique obviously has more chance of succeeding than an opponent who cannot. The axiom is, however, that only sufficient power be used; the greater skill differential, the less the force required to accomplish the technique.

Basically there is little difference between the schools of aikido. In the Uyeshiba school more emphasis is given to the fusion of physical and mental power. Continual reference is made to *ki* or inner power, and initially a great amount of time is given to exercises that will assist in its development. The Uyeshiba student will be taught how to co-ordinate his movements with those of

another so as to bring about a virtual 'dialogue' of movement. He will discipline himself to react at the proper time and not in an ineffective and wild manner. After much practice he will find that he can bring a number of assailants under control, without resorting to brute strength. In fact his aim will be to do so without injuring his opponents. It was Uyeshiba that said, 'Martial training is not training that has as its primary purpose the defeating of others, but the practice of God's love within ourselves.' And this philosophy is basic to all aikido schools.

Students of the Yoshinkan or Shioda system will find slight differences in approach, both ethical and physical, although the basic principles remain the same. Here the emphasis falls on the idea that through the study of correct technique the gentle can control the strong. Instruction follows a set pattern, starting with postural exercises which stress the significance of the positioning of the body's centre of gravity and the avoidance of direct lines of attack. There are also many exercises for developing strong supple joints and limbs. This is followed by the study of the basic controls— i.e. Ikkajo, Nikajo, Sankajo, and Ypnkajo—all concerned with wrist action and holds. Each of these controls has many variations and students soon acquire an extensive repertoire. The Shioda school quotes some hundred and fifty basic techniques which are practised repeatedly. These finally enable the student to master the remaining ones, which total some three thousand in all. Competition is not advocated in the system, as it is considered that aikido goes beyond the concepts of defeat and victory. Emphasis is laid on 'mental harmony'.

The Tomiki school has possibly more adherents than either the Uyeshiba or the Shioda systems, and its distinctive characteristic is that it incorporates competitive situations. Professor Tomiki, after years of study, realized the possibilities aikido offered as a sport. He was very conscious of the fact that aikido had remained a matter of schooling and exercising a series of reflex actions and that other masters had devised their systems on the basis of this pure concept. He believed, however, that man is instinctively competitive, and that even if a competitive element were introduced into aikido the basic principles could still be retained. His competition structure provides students with an opportunity to learn how to co-ordinate their movements with those of another, gives them the chance to evaluate their own ability, and proves to them the effectiveness of the techniques they have studied.

There are four types of competition in Tomiki Aikido, and they are designed to enable a wide age-range to take part. The first is Kata competition, in which competitors can choose which kata they wish to demonstrate. Its purpose is to assess each pair's ability to co-ordinate movement and it involves performing complicated actions in kneeling and standing positions. The whole sequence must be performed in a smooth flowing manner, showing understanding and purpose. Good posture and body control are of paramount importance. A scoring system similar to that in gymnastics is used, with five judges awarding points.

Ninin-dori competition is a free-style event with three players, each of whom in turn takes the part of the defender against the

below Shomen-ate (Push). The first movement of the Randori no Kata, in which the defender has avoided a straight punch to the face by moving inside the attacking arm and projecting the attacker backwards. This he did by applying a hand to the chin and moving in with the body.

bottom Hiki-otoshi (Arm Drop). The seventeenth movement of the Randori no Kata, in which the attacking arm is checked and the defender drops away on to one knee. A key factor of this technique is the use of the attacker's forward impetus.

above Ryote-mochi (Two-handed Throw). By combining a large, circular arm movement with a body turn and drop, the balance of the attacker is broken and he is thrown to the ground. The defender must look to his posture when performing this technique.

above right Gedan-ate (Low Body Projection). The fourth movement of the Randori no Kata, used as a continuation technique against the attacker's resistance to a previous technique.

opposite left Ude-garame (Arm-Lock Throw). The ninth movement of the Randori no Kata has numerous variations and is used as a continuation technique against attempted avoidance of the attacker.

opposite above right Ushiro-muna-dori (Backwards Circle Throw). The attacker attempts to grasp the defender from the rear. The defender immediately brings the attacker into his own centralized position and throws him through the air.

opposite below right Tenchi-nage (Heaven and Earth Throw). A variation of a throw in which the defender's action must be perfectly timed and the body drive co-ordinated with the arm action.

other two. Players are assessed on variation of technique and attack, speed of performance, and general reaction under stress. The overall duration of this event is 3 minutes, and participants have to be extremely fit and not lacking in stamina. Judges watch closely all techniques performed, including how the defender controls the situation presented by the attackers. The attacks must be varied, and the action must be continuous. It is considered bad control if a defender allows both opponents to attack at the same time, unless he can use such a situation to his own advantage. Ninin-dori encourages each participant to become accustomed to being always in a posture from which he can defend himself.

Tanto Randori is a competition giving participants the opportunity of defending themselves against a knife (or short sword), which for the purpose of the event is of rubber. Two players are involved, each in turn acting the part of the defender, who is unarmed, and the attacker, who is armed. The defender scores by demonstrating ability in avoiding the knife attack and applying a skilful aikido technique. The attacker scores by making a positive strike on the target area, which is any part of the trunk between the shoulders and the waist-line. The arms, legs, and face must not be attacked. On completion the player who has scored the highest number of points is announced the winner. The purpose of this competition is to increase reaction speeds and to encourage avoidance by whole-body movement. Good posture and fast, sharp reactions are essential ingredients of this competition.

In Randori Kyoghi two unarmed players compete against each other and attempt to score by applying a skilfully employed aikido technique. If a player scores twice before time is called, he is announced the winner. To participate in this competition with any success, a player must have thoroughly learnt how to co-ordinate his movement with that of another. He must develop a 'feel' for the attacking techniques being employed and an ability to avoid them by good body movement, thus remaining free to produce effective counter-techniques. Action must be continuous,

as non-action – or playing a waiting game – can lead to disqualification. Only senior grades are permitted to enter for this event.

This then is Tomiki Aikido. It gives students the opportunity to study all aspects of aikido, although if a student has no wish to enter competition, he does not have to do so. It will not mar his promotion prospects.

As must be fairly obvious now, the difference between schools is primarily a question of interpretation and application. The basic techniques are similar. It is only the assessment and the proving of effectiveness that differs. On one hand you have a partner co-operating with you, putting up a minimal amount of resistance, and on the other you have co-operation·withdrawn to be replaced by scientific avoidance and resistance.

Grading in aikido

The promotion structure in aikido is similar to that in most other martial arts, being divided into two categories, i.e. kyu grades and dan grades. *Kyu* grades are student grades, rising from the lowest, usually 6th or 5th kyu, to 1st kyu, and they are usually denoted by various coloured belts. *Dan* grades, denoted by a black belt, progress from 1st dan to 8th dan and in rare cases above. In the Uyeshiba and Shioda schools, dan grades wear hakama over their suits, or *gi*. A *hakama* is a divided skirt, which it is said was worn by the samurai whilst practising the martial arts. In the Tomiki school, the wearing of hakama is entirely optional, and very few students feel inclined to wear it, although in the performance of kata it does enhance and add grace to movement.

In the main, students practising Tomiki Aikido in Europe, the USA, and Australia have one syllabus for seniors and another for juniors, a junior being under sixteen years of age. The junior syllabus has nine grades in which different coloured belts are awarded. Locking and twisting techniques are not allowed as the bone structure of juniors can easily be damaged. Emphasis is laid on good posture and movement. In Britain there are 'optional sections'

Tenkai-kote-hineri (Turning Inside Wrist Twist). The ability to defend one's self at all times is essential in aikido. Here (*above*) the defender is on his knees but he has gained a wrist control over his attacker. He then brings his attacker round and down in front of him (*right*), thereby neutralizing his intention.

opposite above left and below Bokken Shiho-nage (Four-quarter Throw against the Sword). During the entry and halfway stage of this technique (*opposite above left*), it is essential that the defender has firm control of the sword and that the attacker is off balance. He must not be allowed to regain any semblance of posture. To complete the throwing action (*opposite below*), the defender continues with his body spin, bringing his own arms down in a sword-like cutting movement to effect a powerful projection of the attacker.

opposite above right Irimi-nage (Entry Technique). A key factor in this technique is to 'enter' with your whole body so that the projection of your opponent is absolute. There are many variations and all should be practised to get complete understanding.

opposite centre right Bokken Mae-otoshi (Arm Push against the Sword). The defender has literally projected the attacker forward by a powerful body turn, using one hand to gain possession of the sword. He must time the body movement precisely for this technique to be accomplished with any success.

in the senior syllabus. Their purpose is to allow those who are not competition-orientated to study the more formal side of aikido, i.e. the *Koryu no Kata*, although they must also have knowledge of the competition rules. Those who enjoy competition may gain promotion points that way, but they must also be fully knowledgeable in the formal side of aikido. Tomiki Aikido is perhaps least developed in Australia, where it has been introduced in the last few years by immigrants from Britain. Uyeshiba Aikido is, however, progressing steadily under the influence of visiting Japanese instructors.

Aikido sessions

Aikido is practised in a *dojo*, or practice hall. Inside is an area, usually square, which is covered by a mat or 'soft floor'. Where possible, certain parts of a dojo are reserved for seating, and the walls behind are used for ceremonial emblems. On entering, students bow in this direction as a sign of respect.

Etiquette and discipline go hand in hand in aikido and certain formalities are carried out at the beginning and end of each

session. When the class has gathered together, the most senior grade present calls the class into line, invariably in order of grade seniority, and the instructor stands in front of them. The senior grade calls 'Seiza' and everyone assumes a seated kneeling position in a set manner.

First the left foot is taken back half a step and the left knee is placed on the mat. Then the right foot is taken back half a step and the right knee is placed on the mat, with the big toes touching each other. The hips are then lowered until the bottom rests on the heels, and the hands are placed lightly on the thighs. The head and trunk are kept upright throughout. Then the senior grade calls 'Rei' and everyone performs a bow, each person placing the hands in front of the knees and bending the trunk forward to an angle of approximately 30 degrees. The neck does not bend, the head does not touch the mat, and the hips are not raised from the heels. In some dojos this action is performed twice, once with the instructor facing the same way as the class, i.e. towards the ceremonial wall, and then with the instructor facing the class.

With this ceremony over, the class starts on a series of 'warming-up' exercises. These usually run to a set pattern and are aimed at conditioning the body. This is followed by basics which intend primarily to teach co-ordination, posture, and good body-alignment. Then specific techniques and various other aspects of aikido are studied. Before the session ends, calming exercises are done, and then comes the finishing ceremony, in which the class is summoned to line again, 'Seiza' is called, and then 'Mokuzo'. Here everyone closes the eyes and concentrates on Misogi or Okinaga, the special breathing exercises. A ceremonial bow completes the lesson. To some Westerners this may seem unnecessary mumbo jumbo. But apart from being formal manners, the breathing in particular does have a beneficial and calming effect.

Bokken Shyomen-ate (Straight Push against the Sword). The defender needs a rapid, smooth movement to the side, combined with a light deflection on the upper part of the sword blade (*above*), to avoid this straight thrust to the throat. At the same time (*right*), he uses his free hand to strike at the attacker's head. The key factor in this part of the technique is to ensure that the strike is combined with a strong hip action.

opposite *Bokken Oshi-taioshi* (Elbow Push against the Sword). Another technique in which the sword is taken away from the attacker, this requires firm control and perfect timing. The projection is brought about by a strong pushing action against the attacker's elbow and the hilt of the sword, with the whole body being used as the driving force.

Bokken Tori (Body Sword Technique). The defender starts to take the sword away from the attacker (*above*). The avoiding action by the defender has to be perfectly timed, as in all techniques of defence against the sword. In the second picture (*right*), the cutting edge of the sword has been drawn up from the attacker's groin to the throat. In practice, the attacker is thrown backwards from this action.

Aikido and self-defence

To varying extents all the martial arts lay claim to effectiveness as a means of self-defence. Aikido literature is certainly no exception. However, a practitioner would need to be very experienced for aikido to be an effective self-defence system. Many police forces certainly give instruction in aikido as part of their self-defence curriculum, but the techniques employed vary slightly from what the average student would be taught. All this, however, is to ignore the basic philosophy of aikido, which advocates non-violent control and the neutralization of any form aggression may take. Self-defence, on the other hand, may begin as an attempt to block an attack but it invariably crosses the thin dividing line between defence and offence. True aikido, in other words, does not claim to be a method of self-defence, and no practitioner would presume to say that it was a better system than any of the other martial arts.

The new skills of aikido

The amount of time it takes to become proficient at aikido naturally varies, frequency of practice obviously being one factor, but all syllabuses demand that a student practises for a specific number of hours before entering for the various grades. Aikido is simple when you know how, but obtaining the know-how is initially very difficult.

A major reason for this is that it is a natural human reaction to become tense when confronted with an aggressive action. Proof of this can be had by flicking a hand at someone's eyes. The invariable reaction is to protect oneself by raising the hands and moving the head back. In so doing one immediately places oneself in a worse position, from the point of view of defence. The jerking back of the head could cause one to assume an unstable stance, and the raising of the hands to the face obstructs the vision. This reaction must therefore be unlearned.

It is accomplished by teaching students to stand in a good, sound

Jo Gyakugamae-ate (Reverse Throw against the Jo). Here the defender moves outside the attacking thrust and catches the *jo*, or stick, in one hand, while the other strikes at the attacker's head. The key factor of this technique is the stretching action of the chest.

Jo Shomen-ate (Push against the Jo). Having avoided the spear-like attack by moving inside the attacker's circle of movement, the defender keeps firm control of the jo with one hand, while the other pushes under the attacker's chin. This push is co-ordinated with a forward-driving movement of the body.

posture and to move well and with the whole body when avoiding the direct line of attack. They are taught that to move the body freely, they must be in a relaxed state, so time is spent in getting the student 'conditioned'. The above may sound an easy thing to accomplish, but the co-ordination required is much more complex than it seems.

Another instinctive reaction which must be untaught is the attempt to stop the force of an attack by meeting it 'head on'. If you are physically tough and in a strong posture, you may for a time get away with it, but all that will be accomplished is the stopping of the force, not the intention to attack. By standing there in that manner you will automatically be tense and you will therefore find it difficult to react appropriately.

You must therefore be taught to put your body into motion immediately you perceive any aggressive action. The fact that you

below Entry for Jo Mae-otoshi. Note the deep avoidance movement, which is a key factor in this technique.

below right Jo Mae-otoshi (Arm Push against the Jo). After avoiding a thrusting attack, the defender quickly spins in, traps the attacker's arm, and with a forward body-movement throws the attacker.

are moving will ensure a relaxed state, and this is where your technique begins. As the attack reaches contact distance, you commence avoidance, which should, in nearly every case, be a circular movement. The next step is to bring about the unbalancing of the attacker either by manual means or by causing him to overextend. Without stable foundation he cannot resist and you then apply a throw or an immobilizing control. Most importantly, the sequence from start to finish must 'flow'. Neither your motion nor the attacker's should stop until you have applied either the

throw or the immobilization. If it does, you give him an opportunity to regain stability and begin a fresh attack.

Judging distance is another complex skill that has to be learnt. In aikido the approximate distance between players is two arms' length apart. At that distance and by watching your opponent's eyes you can take in the whole of his body. In closer-contact sports, such as judo, the attacking movement is perhaps felt rather than seen. But in aikido, more often than not, you perceive the attacking action by sight and it is therefore necessary for you to be aware of every part of the attacker's body. However, weapons, i.e. knife, short sword, bo, and long sword, may also be used, and these vary in length as well as direction of attack. Your distance must therefore be flexible and adjusted according to circumstances. All weapons must be treated as an extension of your opponent's arm, and your contact distance moves to the end of the weapon nearest to you and your avoidance begins there.

One skill that must align itself to the judging of distance is speed, an essential element in aikido. Although the attacker's momentum must be assessed and will in many ways dictate the action you take, you have to train yourself to vary your own speed of movement. At times it has to be a lot faster than your opponent's. Speed means not only reaction time, but the ability to reduce or extend the distance between yourself and your opponent. Part of your training will therefore aim to develop speed of acceleration. A sense of timing must also be acquired. To have good timing is to have the ability to harmonize your own movement with that of your opponent, in other words to react in the correct manner to the actions of your attacker.

opposite below   Jo Irimi-nage (Jo Entering Technique). The attacker thrusts at the defender, who moves in to throw, but the attacker avoids this by retreating backwards (*below left*). To overcome this avoidance (*below right*), the defender moves in the same direction as the attacker and by use of the jo throws him backwards.

below left   Jo Shyomen-tsuki (Straight Thrust with the Jo). This jo technique is applied after an attempt by the attacker to wrest the jo from the defender. Its action is similar to that of *Sumi-otoshi*, but with a greater emphasis on large body movement to overcome the added leverage of using the jo. A strong downward sword-cutting action is required to accomplish the projection of the attacker.

below   Jo Tentaii Mae-otoshi (Circular Drop against the Jo). The defender has avoided a thrusting attack with the jo by using a large turning movement. He then catches the jo and, with a co-ordinated movement of arms and body, projects the attacker through the air.

top *Jo Kote-mawashi* (Inside Twist with the Jo). The action here is to unbalance the attacker immediately the jo is grasped. Then a circular movement with the jo traps the attacker's wrist, and the defender's end of the jo is raised and thrust towards the attacker. The twist and pain of the trapped wrist cause the attacker to be thrown.

above *Jo Shiho-nage* (Four-quarter Throw with the Jo). A similar body and arm action to the technique used for taking away the sword, but the stress must be laid on perfect co-ordination of the body and arm movements.

Judgement of distance, speed, and timing are the three basic requirements for a well co-ordinated *aikidoka*, or follower of aikido. An important element in accomplishing these skills is the maintenance of good posture. In aikido you must assume a posture conducive to the ability to move quickly in any direction. This means good body-alignment, and good alignment demands that the centre of gravity remains over the body's support base.

The basic posture assumed in aikido is with one foot in front of the other, approximately shoulder width apart, knees relaxed and with the forward knee slightly bent so that on looking down you cannot see the big toe of the advanced foot. Hips should be square; the head and trunk upright and relaxed. The aim is to have a strong, sound posture, with a feeling of relaxed, fluid mobility.

The hips play an important part in posture as they do in aikido movement as a whole. When correctly used, the power coming from them via the trunk to the arms is considerable. Much perseverance and practice is needed to acquire this technique, but it is nevertheless essential. Hip power can be lessened by wrong use of the shoulder, but if the hips are kept square the chances of this happening are reduced. In movement, especially turning, the hips should lead, as the hip circle is obviously smaller than the shoulder circle, shoulders being wider than hips. A number of the basic exercises performed at the beginning of each aikido training period are devoted to the correct use of hips.

The hands and arms also play an intrinsic part in aikido technique. The fingers are kept extended except, of course, when grasping or holding. Then the grip is similar to that used when holding a sword, and power is exerted mainly through the little finger rather than the forefinger and thumb. The arms are kept more or less straight, but not stiff. Their position will vary between low (*gedan*), central (*chudan*), and high (*jodan*), according to the attack situation being offered. In all positions power is concentrated in the little-finger edge of the hand.

The philosophy of aikido

Quite a large number of aikido students, primarily in the West, manage to progress without involving themselves in the mental/spiritual side of the subject, although it may initially have been one reason for taking up the art. However, aikido does have certain positive links with Eastern philosophy, particularly Zen. Zen gives the centre for meditation and seat of 'mental power' as the *tanden*, which is a point situated about $1\frac{1}{2}$ inches below the navel. This centre, the *saitten-no-ten*, is stressed as the power source in the teaching of aikido. Several names are given to the power, the most common being *ki* or inner energy. A more Western interpretation of this inner energy, or keeping centre, is perhaps the ability to maintain good body-alignment and to concentrate one's power in the required direction. But certainly in both the Uyeshiba and the Yoshinkan schools students are made aware of this power, and exercises such as the unbendable arm are given to develop it. Special breathing techniques, sitting still, and meditation become an intrinsic part of their training. That a certain amount of mystique has grown up around it is true. This is a pity because it is an

above   *Jo Ashi-barai* (Low Sweep with the Jo). The key factors of this technique are the initial unbalancing of the attacker and a perfectly timed sweeping-action against both his legs, causing him to be thrown on to his back. This is a very spectacular technique if performed correctly.

left   *Jo Ude-garame* (Arm-lock Throw with the Jo). The attacker's whole arm is trapped by the jo in this technique, and a strong body-action on the part of the defender projects the attacker through the air. Any resistance by the attacker to this technique could cause dislocation of both elbow and shoulder joint.

essential part of aikido training, although it must be admitted that not all instructors are as knowledgeable in this respect as they might be.

Another important principle in aikido is that of non-resistance. It was Professor Uyeshiba who demonstrated this quality most clearly. It was said of him that his every movement was in accord with the laws of nature, and that he thereby attained a state of absolute non-resistance. In aikido non-resistance is not only a physical thing, it also has mental/spiritual overtones. To a Westerner 'pliable' is perhaps a better way to describe the state, although the word should imply mental as well as physical pliability. If you are pushed you go with the push, and if you are pulled you go with the pull, thereby blending with your opponent's movement and direction of power. Such pliability has to be practised, because it is instinctive to react against a push by pushing back or against a pull by pulling back. You have to learn to overcome this natural reaction by never clashing with an opponent's force and by using your circular movements to be pliable and turn his force against him. You have to learn to lead him into your own sphere and thereby bring him under control.

Aikido for women

Very little has been said about this aspect of aikido. There is, however, most certainly a place for women in the art. In most clubs there is no separation of the sexes, either in practice or in grading standards. There is no age limit and both young and old may safely participate because of the non-aggressive philosophy involved. Expertise is judged on technical ability, not strength.

In Tomiki Aikido women need not engage in either Tanto Randori or Randori Kyoghi; indeed they are encouraged to participate in a gentler version in which resistance is minimal. The purpose of unsegregated participation is to help them understand and perfect their techniques in a more realistic environment. In the various koryus, where gracefulness of movement and technical expertise are most valuable, women certainly hold their own. Mixed practice is also doubly beneficial. It teaches a woman to overcome a physically stronger person by sheer movement, and it teaches a man to adapt his techniques and thereby follow the basic principle of aikido.

One British woman, a 4th dan, summed it up when she said: *The choice of Aikido out of all the martial arts for me, as a woman, was the sheer effectiveness of it, and the fact that this skill can be acquired without muscle power or loss of gracefulness.*

How to join a club

If after reading this you decide to study aikido, choose your club carefully. When you hear of one that might suit you, pay it a visit and watch aikido being practised. This way you should soon discover whether it is a reputable club, catering for all levels of student. Assess the atmosphere; do the students seem to be enjoying a well-disciplined, interesting, and well-planned lesson? A short chat with the instructor and some of the students should give you an inkling whether you will fit in.

Tetsu Ehara 5th Dan, demonstrating variations of *Hiki-otoshi* (*above*) and *Kote-gaeshi* (*left*). In the former, it is essential that the attacker's impetus and power is turned to the defender's advantage. Note there is no 'sleeve pull', as would occur in the similar judo technique. In the latter note the power of the circle Ehara makes as he turns the attacker's wrist outwards.

When first starting aikido, be prepared to meet some frustrating periods when nothing seems to go right; this happens in most courses of study. You must persevere. Some start aikido and after a few lessons give up: they find it is perhaps too laborious or too complex. It is complex at first—what skill is not? Bear in mind that to learn and understand anything, you must see the whole, not just a part. There is something in aikido for everyone. All age groups can benefit and you will certainly feel better both physically and mentally.

A word of advice: beware of the place which offers 'quick grades'. There are no short cuts. Remember that the instructor cannot do it all for you. Only by long diligent practice and perseverance will you improve. The promotion structure is there to assist in evaluating your ability and progress, and it creates an incentive to learning. The grades themselves are relatively unimportant. They are not status symbols there to enhance ego. The only true evaluation of your ability and skill must come from yourself.

Have fun, study and practise hard, and above all enjoy your aikido. Then you will succeed.

Karate-do

The origins of karate can be traced back through the centuries from modern Japan via Okinawa to China and possibly to India in the fourth and fifth centuries BC. Much of this history is documented, whilst some is embedded in myth and romance. Whether fact or fiction, however, it has had a strong influence upon the attitudes of *karateka*, or students of karate, and it provides an illuminating insight into a fighting art which has also recently evolved into a sport.

Yoga, for example, has had an effect upon karate in general and its breathing patterns in particular, and it is believed to have originated in the Indus Valley about the fifth century BC. Karateka place special emphasis on the need to develop powerful diaphragms and one of the methods they use to achieve this is yoga-type strong diaphragmatic breathing. By powerful exhalations focused on the diaphragm, muscle contraction is intensified and power boosted.

Tradition relates that these techniques were brought to China by a Buddhist monk named Bhodidharma (in Chinese) or Daruma (in Japanese) in the sixth century AD. Legend has it that he founded the monastery of Shaolin-Szu (Shorin-ji in Japanese) in the province of Hu-nan. To Bhodidharma are also attributed the origins of Zen Buddhism (a branch of Buddhism later to achieve its fullest flowering in Japan) and a form of physical training which was to become the basis of kung fu and karate. Although kung fu and karate are now considered distinct arts, they might more appropriately be described as branches of the same tree, the roots of which can be traced back possibly to Bhodidharma and certainly to China. Finding that his students lacked both the physical and mental stamina to withstand the rigours of Zen, Bhodidharma devised a system of physical training to develop these qualities. This system involved a combination of Indian yoga breathing-techniques and native Chinese unarmed combat known as *kempo*.

As a result of Bhodidharma's training methods, the monks of Shaolin-Szu became as famous throughout China for their fighting skill as for their Buddhist knowledge. The Chinese were highly advanced in the field of medicine, their acupuncture cures demonstrating a knowledge of the various nerve centres of the body, and kempo benefited by being able to apply its fighting techniques to those vulnerable points. As the techniques spread throughout that vast and varied country, they gradually assumed

opposite *Yoko-tobi-geri* (Flying Side Kick). A jumping kick to the head normally used as a surprise attack, it may have derived from techniques designed to bring down a mounted horseman.

different forms according to the local conditions. The short, stocky paddyfield workers of the south, with their strong upper bodies, naturally emphasized arm and head techniques. In contrast the nomadic horsemen of North China, having developed strong legs, gave precedence to kicking and jumping. The origins of the different styles of kung fu and karate were already apparent. The northern Chinese styles also strongly influenced the development of neighbouring Korean karate or *tae kwon do*.

Although we know that Shaolin-Szu existed and was in fact burned to the ground on two occasions, there is no positive proof concerning the existence of Bhodidharma. Some people believe that he is merely a literary invention to satisfy the traditional Chinese requirement of a story to explain the origins of a custom. Others think that he is a kaleidoscopic image or amalgam of many people, each of whom contributed to the development of Zen and Chinese kempo. In general, however, both Chinese and Japanese historians appear to accept that he did exist.

Stretching southwards from Japan to Taiwan (Formosa) are the islands of the Ryukyu chain, which provide natural stepping-stones for Chinese cultural and commercial influence. The largest of these islands is Okinawa, which in many respects has been the meeting ground of Chinese and Japanese cultures. It was to this island that kempo was eventually carried by Chinese émigrés and where it underwent further changes.

Combat techniques known as *te* (hand) had existed for many centuries in Okinawa but they were traditionally of a hard, square nature whereas the Chinese systems were of a softer, more flowing and rounded form. These contrasting elements were to combine and assume a new name, tang hand, 'tang' being the name of a Chinese dynasty which was used loosely to mean China in general.

Politically, Okinawa was subject for long periods to Japanese domination. This domination was characteristically severe and included the illegalizing of weapons for the general public. The effect of this, however, was to encourage the clandestine development of tang hand and the adaptation of agricultural implements for defensive and offensive purposes, as described in the Okinawan weaponry section.

The traditional clothing of the occupying Japanese soldiery was wooden armour and to strike effectively through this with empty hands required substantial foot and hand conditioning. The development of hand calluses was therefore emphasized, and to this day Okinawan styles of karate place greater emphasis on hand conditioning than do most Japanese styles. As Okinawan fighting was less class based than that in hierarchic Japan, and as Buddhism was never particularly popular in Okinawa, there was also much less 'philosophizing' associated with it than was to become the case in Japan. In Okinawa it was purely and simply a form of combat.

Different forms of tang hand evolved in different parts of Okinawa and, following an Okinawan tour by the present Japanese emperor, the leader of one style, Funakoshi Gichin, was in 1917 invited to Japan by the Ministry of Education to give demonstrations. All his early presentations were to groups of intellectuals. These

A block from a crouching position. Crouching, as opposed to jumping, techniques are particularly representative of styles with a southern, as opposed to northern, Chinese influence.

To punch something hard, without hesitation or inhibition, requires that the hand be properly conditioned. Some karate styles develop substantial calluses to act as protection and to prevent cutting of the skin.

were so well received that in 1923 he returned to take up permanent residence in Japan. At first Funakoshi hired judo and kendo halls for his clubs, but such was their popularity that in 1936 he eventually opened a permanent *dojo* or hall. This became known as the 'Shotokan' or Shoto's house or hall, Shoto being Funakoshi's pen-name. Shotokan was also eventually to become the name of the style he practised.

Other Okinawans soon followed Funakoshi to Japan, including Chojun Miyagi, founder of the Goju style. However, peculiarly Japanese styles also began to emerge; for example Yamaguchi Gogen, a Japanese student of Miyagi's, created his own interpretation of Goju, and Hironori Otsuka, having incorporated certain ju-jutsu elements, created the Wado style. This increasing Japanese element within karate is reflected in the change of name that occurred in 1936. In that year Funakoshi abandoned the name 'tang hand' and substituted the word 'karate'. Doubtless the timing of this change was influenced by the increasing nationalism and growing anti-Chinese feeling within Japan, which were the following year to lead

top A punching board, or *makiwara*, is used to develop proper punching technique and to toughen and condition the hands.

above *Neko-ashi-dachi* (Cat Stance). A narrow-based stance with the weight mainly on the rear foot. The front foot, poised lightly on the ball, aids rapid movement and facilitates quick, flicking kicks.

to war. As 'tang' was a word obviously identifiable with China, its use within Japan was naturally increasingly unpopular. Although this change of name was at first resented by the other Okinawan traditionalists, it eventually came to be accepted by all. 'Karate' is in fact a Japanese word meaning 'empty hand' and, quite apart from being nationally acceptable, it was also descriptive, not only in the obvious physical sense but also in the more subtle Zen sense of 'emptiness'. Funakoshi put it thus:

As a mirror's polished surface reflects whatever stands before it and a quiet valley carries even small sounds so must the student of Karate render his mind empty of selfishness and wickedness in an effort to react appropriately to anything he might encounter. This is the meaning of Kara or 'empty' in Karate.

The implications of this statement are quite complex. It obviously suggests a moral responsibility not to exploit potentially lethal skills for personal gain or gratification. However, there is more than that in it. In Zen 'emptiness' implies the negation of conscious thought and the substitution of instinctive response. In other words, the karateka strives to employ consciously acquired techniques only in so far as they have been totally absorbed and are therefore no longer conscious. By training to the point of instinctiveness, the expert karateka is conscious of the essence of a situation rather than the minor and irrelevant detail. He watches the whole of his opponent's body rather than the parts—the hands or the legs—and he sees the wood rather than the trees. Neither is he consciously working out tactics, thinking, 'If he does this, I will do that.' By the time he had consciously analysed the situation the opportunity to act appropriately would have vanished. Responses must therefore be instinctive and immediate. Ideally 'all is emptiness—even the thought of emptiness is no longer there. From this absolute emptiness comes the most wondrous enfoldment of doing.'

Thus, unlike most of the other Japanese martial arts, karate is not in the direct Japanese Zen or samurai tradition, although it has in the present century assumed a similar veneer. Its leading practitioners undoubtedly see themselves in the same historical tradition as that of the other martial arts. Being Japanese, they identify with their nation's history and its philosophical attitudes and, to some extent, the techniques have been adapted to fit into that pattern. Samurai and Zen attitudes, whilst not having a great historical depth in karate, are nonetheless real in the minds of many of its practitioners. Being great adapters, the Japanese have made karate their own and incorporated within it their own philosophies.

At the end of the Second World War under the American occupation, the teaching of all *budo*, or martial ways, was forbidden. However, possibly due to its less nationalist associations, this does not appear to have been applied as rigidly to karate as to the other arts. Funakoshi reopened his club in 1947 and endeavoured to create an all-style organization called the Japan Karate Association. When other groups were unwilling to collaborate, however, it became confined to his own style, which then assumed the name Shotokan. The other instructors developed their own schools and as the popularity of karate spread to the West, particularly in the late 1960s and early 1970s, Japanese instructors moved overseas. It was during this period that an increasing 'sport' element evolved, designed to cater for popular demand both in Japan and abroad. With them, these instructors brought to the West substantial technical skills. Unfortunately, they also exported an organizational chaos which is described later under the heading 'Modern problems facing karate'.

The dojo

As with the other Japanese martial arts, the place at which one practises karate is known as the *dojo*. Literally translated, 'dojo' means 'way place', the place at which one practises one's way. With the Zen implication of 'way to enlightenment', the word obviously suggests more than 'gymnasium' with its purely physical associations. In appearance a dojo is generally nothing more than a bare hall with a wooden floor. As there are few throws in karate, it does not contain the floor matting used for judo and aikido.

In a very traditional dojo there may be a small Shinto or Zen shrine. Most modern dojos are more likely to contain an association symbol or a picture of the founder on the end wall towards which, as a sign of respect, the students bow on entering and leaving the dojo. Many dojos are also very Japanese-orientated and display the Japanese national flag. At one end there may be punching bags, punching balls, weights, and large mirrors to help with training and the personal analysis of technique.

Karateka wear loose-fitting white suits called *gi*, fastened with a coloured belt indicating the grade of the wearer. The student, or *kyu*, belt colours vary from association to association but all the instructor, or *dan*, grades wear a black belt. Although it is not indicated in the belt colour, the senior dan grades are also arranged in a hierarchy rising from 1st dan to 8th or 10th dan, according to the association concerned. The most senior grade is reserved for the senior man of that style in the world. The hierarchy of student grades is in reverse order, with the lowest grade being 10th kyu and the most senior 1st kyu. Although the belt colours do vary somewhat from association to association, the following break-down is the most common:

white	beginners, 10th and 9th kyu
light blue	8th and 7th kyu
yellow	6th and 5th kyu
green	4th and 3rd kyu
brown	2nd and 1st kyu

The atmosphere within a dojo is generally very formal and the instructor is referred to as *sensei* (teacher) rather than by his first name. This formality assists club discipline and perhaps surprisingly, in the informal West, it is not in the least unpopular. Japanese terminology is also used to describe technique and equipment.

Basic principles of karate

In the execution of any sport or fighting form there are always certain basic principles which apply. Some, although not all of these, are in fact applicable to all sports and even to daily living. For example, the relationships between muscular relaxation and

Zenkutsu-dachi (Forward Stance). This broad-based, firmly positioned stance permits full rear-leg thrust and hip rotation. The non-punching arm pulls back simultaneously to increase hip rotation and add power to the punch.

top Kotutsu-dachi (Backward Stance). This is a defensive position well suited to blocking attacks from the front. By moving the body, and hence the centre of gravity, forward, counter attacks can also be easily launched.

above Kiba-dachi (Horse Stance). So named because of its similarity to a horse-riding posture, this strong stance is particularly suited to attacks to the side, such as the Uraken (Back-fist Strike).

potential speed of movement or between relaxation and breathing habits are obviously not peculiar to karate or even just to sport. Both are equally applicable to the housewife or to the man on the factory floor. Some of these basic principles are described here as they apply to karate.

Stance The way in which one stands obviously influences the actions one can immediately take. A very broad-based stance with a low centre of gravity is extremely stable and good for launching powerful punches and blocks, but it is not good for rapid movement. On the other hand, a narrow based stance with a high centre of gravity is suited to quick movements but not to powerful punching. As some styles stress speed whereas others emphasize power, the characteristic stance of each style reflects the dominant principle.

Some styles are also very stable to the front or rear, whilst being relatively weak to the side. The Backwards Stance (Kotutsu-dachi), for example, is a defensive position in which the direction of potential thrust is primarily to the front.

The Horse Stance (Kiba-dachi) is particularly suited to strong sideways techniques such as the Back-fist Strike (Uraken).

A stance such as the Hourglass Stance (Hangetsu-dachi), in which the feet are virtually screwed into the ground thereby creating friction, is good for sideways thrusts as well as stability.

All stances have their own in-built advantages and disadvantages, and the all-round karateka must acquire a broad repertoire so that he can instinctively adopt the one that is suited to the situation. Being of fundamental importance, a good stance is the first thing taught at almost every club.

Power and speed The power of a moving body depends upon its mass and velocity. To achieve full power, whatever one's mass or weight, one must be properly positioned, i.e. by adopting a good, sound stance. Apart from ensuring that impact can be withstood, this enables full use to be made of the powerful rear-leg thrust and co-ordinated hip rotation. This thrust and rotation can then be transferred via the trunk to the striking arm. Being much lighter than the leg, the arm is potentially weaker but, provided it is kept relaxed and tension avoided, it is capable of considerable speed of movement. With proper co-ordination, therefore, full use can be made of one's weight, as represented by the leg and trunk, and speed, as represented by the arms, and maximum power thereby achieved.

The rotary movement of the hips and its effect upon the fist might be likened to the action of a whip. This is particularly noticeable in the Roundhouse Strike (Mawashi-zuki), although it also applies to straight punches such as the Fore-fist Punch. The speed of the tip of the whip (i.e. the fist) moves in direct proportion to that of the handle (i.e. the hips). Similarly, the faster a discus thrower rotates his hips, the faster his discus moves and the further he can throw it.

Relaxation, however, is vital for both the discus thrower and the karateka. The effect of tension would be similar to that of using a

long stiff pole instead of a flexible whip, and maximum acceleration would not be achieved. It is only at the last possible moment on focus or impact that tension is applied. The entire body is then tensed, firming up the karateka's joints and converting the tip of his 'whip' into a firmly supported but rapidly moving hammer. It is through the effective application of this technique, and by developing hands which are sufficiently hardened to withstand impact, that karateka are able to perform the brick- or ice-breaking techniques which are so often viewed by spectators with incredulity and disbelief. The breaking is not a trick. It is simply an application of a power-generating technique.

This principle of hip rotation and speed naturally applies to all styles, although interpretation varies from one style to another.

top left Hangetsu-dachi (Hourglass Stance). From this stance, a downward block and a Back-fist Strike are being performed simultaneously against two assailants.

top right and above Mawashi-zuki (Roundhouse Strike). Delivered with the side of the hand (or knife hand), the Roundhouse Strike rotates around the elbow and is aimed at the temple, neck, or collar bone.

The broad-based, powerful Shotokan stance on the left contrasts with the narrower, speed-motivated Shukokai stance on the right. The hand positions are also typical.

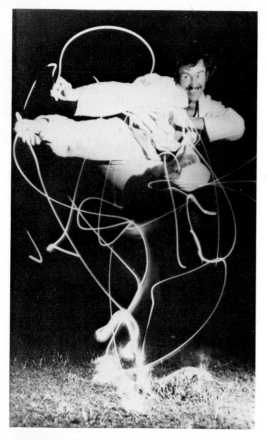

Shotokan, which is basically a power style using broad stances, places great emphasis on rear-leg drive and full-hip rotation. Shukokai, on the other hand, being designed for competition, is keen to get its blow in first rather than to emphasize power. It therefore keeps the hips relatively square to the opponent, thus bringing the rear foot and fist into a closer position for striking. Speed is generated via a whip-like double movement of the hips but the powerful rear-leg thrust is largely sacrificed. Both are perfectly sensible interpretations designed for a specific need.

Focus and kiai The point of imaginary contact in karate is known as 'focus'. This is the moment at which the body is tensed and speed is converted into power. A *kiai*, or yell, which comes more from the diaphragm than the throat, accompanies the action. Its effect is to assist muscle contraction, to stabilize the joints, and to enable one to concentrate all one's physical and mental energies on a given point at a given time. And it can have a frightening or at least distracting effect upon the opponent too. This is not its prime purpose, but in competition momentary distraction can be enough to create a point-scoring opportunity.

Zanshin In order to avoid distraction, karateka should develop the mental state of *zanshin*, or what the Japanese refer to as an all-seeing 'mind like the moon'. This involves a state of total and unemotional awareness, which incorporates perception not just through the eyes but through an intuition born of experience and training. Fully developed, it can be used to achieve psychological domination over opponents.

Some techniques and their applications
Unlike judo, which is basically a throwing, locking, strangulation, and groundwork method of combat, and aikido, which mainly involves projections or throws off the wrist utilizing the opponent's movements to one's own advantage, karate is primarily a punching and kicking form. Again, unlike boxing, where only the fist is used for punching, karate employs a very large range of body parts and in fact virtually any hard bony part of the body can act as striker. Each part can also be used in a wide variety of ways, in the same or different formations.

For example, in a *Seiken*, a straightforward Fore-fist Punch to the opponent's body or face, the arm thrusts forward in a straight line, contact being made through the knuckles of the index and adjacent finger. With a similar formation but with the wrist slightly bent, the fist can rotate in an arc around the elbow in a fast snapping action to make contact through the back of the same two knuckles and we have a very different and effective surprise technique known as the Back-fist Strike or Uraken. This can be used to strike forward, sideways, or to the rear and is normally employed to attack soft parts of the body such as the face, solar plexus, or groin.

There follows a selection of the many other different techniques available. Only one application of each is illustrated, but, as with the fist, several different applications are normally possible.

opposite above   Lights attached to the hands and feet of a karateka demonstrate the speed at which a series of punches, kicks, and blocks can be performed. The camera shutter was open for 3 seconds.

opposite centre   By keeping relaxed, the striking fist can, immediately before focus, be moving very fast. Through proper breathing, a good stance, and kiai, the entire body is then tensed and speed is converted into power.

opposite below   *Uraken* (Back-fist Strike). Here a downward block is followed by a Back-fist Strike to the jaw. Unlike punches, in which the fist travels in a straight line, strikes are performed by moving the fist in a rotary movement or arc around the elbow.

left   *Nukite* (Spear-hand Thrust). Thrusts are attacks with the tips of the fingers to soft parts of the body. Unlike strikes, but as with punches, they travel in a straight line.

Koken (Back of Wrist). On this occasion it is being used to block a lunge punch.

Taisho (Palm Heel). Here a deflecting block with the left hand is followed by a palm-heel attack to the jaw.

opposite above Empi (Elbow) and *Sokuto* (Knife Foot). Both are being used here—to fend off different assailants.

opposite below left Hiza-geri (Knee). On this occasion, the knee is used to attack an assailant moving in with a lowered head, possibly for a head butt. The arms can also pull the head down on to the knee.

opposite below right Atama (Head). Any hard, bony part of the body can be used for striking—including the head.

left Koshi (Ball of Foot). This time the kick is used to attack the jaw. Speed is developed by keeping the leg bent until the last moment and power derives from the full hip thrust. The toes of the kicking foot are curled up to avoid injury.

below Ushiro-geri (Back Kick). A surprise long-range attack to the body or head, this is one of the few techniques in which the upper body is not kept upright.

Kata

The number of techniques, even basic techniques, in any particular style, is considerable and learning them can present a problem. Apart from individual punches, kicks, or blocks, a style can include combinations of hand and foot techniques, changes of pace, special breathing patterns, maintenance of balance, and modification in muscle tension, etc. Each technique is generally first learned by itself and practised repeatedly either alone or in groups of students. This repetition of individual techniques is known as *kihon*.

When the elements of each of a number of individual techniques have been grasped, they are strung together in a fixed sequence known as a *kata* and practised in combination. One of the great kata originators was Funakoshi Gichin. A kata is basically a series of attacking and defensive movements, taking the form of an imaginary fight with several opponents approaching from different directions. Practised without opponents, the movements are highly formalized but they do become second nature so that in a subsequent self-defence situation they tend to be applied instinctively. Practised with opponents, the applications of the movements are immediately obvious. Most styles have about five basic kata which together include the basic techniques. There are, however, many more advanced katas and several styles have as many as fifty kata.

The practice of kata particularly encourages technical analysis and control of movement. It is therefore extremely useful for developing good form. To many traditionalists it is much more in the

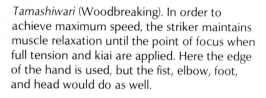

Tamashiwari (Woodbreaking). In order to achieve maximum speed, the striker maintains muscle relaxation until the point of focus when full tension and kiai are applied. Here the edge of the hand is used, but the fist, elbow, foot, and head would do as well.

142

genuine tradition of karate than is competition, which inevitably has many restrictive rules and is therefore considered by some to be artificial. In contrast, kata performance permits all techniques to be practised with maximum commitment and effort, and total identification with the movement is possible. Perhaps regretfully, competition has the greater appeal in the Western world and kata, whilst not being in danger of extinction, certainly takes a secondary and somewhat academic position in general karate interest.

Woodbreaking

The extent to which wood, tile, stone or ice breaking is practised in karate clubs varies considerably according to style. All would agree that a good karateka should be capable of breaking, but most styles would consider that this achievement is the natural outcome of properly executed techniques and need not be given any particular emphasis within the club programme. In general, therefore, it is much less practised than is generally supposed although, as it obviously has a popular appeal, it is often incorporated in public demonstrations.

Some styles, notably Kyokushinkai, do include it as part of their grading system and a student is required to break a specified thickness of wood before being promoted to the related grade. The purpose of this is to prove unequivocally that he is capable of breaking and does not have inhibitions about hitting something hard. It is therefore a trial or a test, and literally translated 'tamashiwari', the Japanese word for woodbreaking, means 'trial by wood'.

Breaking should obviously be practised only under proper supervision. Improperly executed and without adequate hand conditioning, it could lead to serious injury.

Competition

Jiu-kumite or free-style competition is a post-war and extremely popular development. It does, however, convert karate from what is basically a *budo* (martial way) form into a sport and as such it has its opponents as well as its advocates. Its strongest opponents believe that it totally distorts karate's basic philosophy and objectives. They consider it to be artificial, lacking in lethality, and contrary to the samurai spirit with which they tend to identify. Such critics place greater emphasis on the practice of kata and basic techniques.

Even amongst those styles that do take part in competition there are still considerable differences within their respective rules. All exclude the more obviously lethal techniques, such as kicks to the groin, and open-hand techniques, such as finger attacks to the eyes. However, the degree of contact permitted varies from style to style. In general the no-contact rule applies, and attacks, whilst being fully focused, should nevertheless stop just short of the opponent. Despite this, different styles tend to interpret 'contact' with varying degrees of severity.

Kyokushinkai, on the other hand, do permit full contact in some of their competitions. Punches and kicks to the body are allowed as the musculature of the upper body can be built up sufficiently to

top One of the four corner judges carefully watching a tournament.

above Tatsuo Suzuki demonstrates a Roundhouse Kick.

withstand them. Kicks, but not punches, to the head are also allowed, the former being permitted on the grounds that, as the leg is relatively slow moving and has far to travel, it should be possible to block it. Face punches are not allowed as, due to their potential speed, they are very difficult to block and cause the greatest number of injuries. Kyokushinkai believe in the 'one punch, one kick will finish the fight' philosophy. Theirs is very much a budo, rather than a sport, approach and in training they often use protective padding.

In an attempt to place karate on an international and competitive basis, the Federation of All Japan Karate-do Organisations (FAJKO) after its formation in 1964 set about creating competitive rules of a non-contact nature which would allow inter-style competition. By the early 1970s these had been largely accepted and the first all-style world championship was held in Tokyo in 1970.

Competitions are held in an area 8 metres square and are controlled by a referee who moves freely within the area, assisted by four judges seated at the corners. There may also be a controller, whom the referee can consult if he wishes. Final responsibility lies with the referee, although in certain circumstances the controller may ask him to reconsider his decision. In view of the split-second judgements required of karate referees, the quality of official is obviously of prime importance. Weak officiating can lead to potentially dangerous situations and an escalation in contact.

Competitions normally last for 3 minutes, with the possibility of 2-minute extensions in the case of a draw. The scoring area consists of the entire head and the front and back of the trunk. The contestant's aim is to get a fully focused blow to the target area. If the blow is perfectly executed (i.e. it has good focus, balance, kiai, etc.) and stops fractionally short of contact, the referee will stop the bout, shout 'Ippon' (full point), raise his hand in the air in the direction of the scorer, and the contest will end immediately. If it is a good but not perfect blow, he will award a half point and the contest will continue. Two half points count as one full point and finish the match on the spot. If a blow is not properly controlled and the opponent is struck, the striker may receive a disqualification or a warning. If the fight continues for the full 3 minutes and neither contestant is ahead on points, extra time may be allowed or the referee, assisted by the judges, may decide the contest, taking into account skill, fighting spirit, and attitude.

In order to make bouts both more adventuresome and more interesting for spectators, an increasing number of competitions are being held over the full 3 minutes with the total number of points scored per competitor determining the winner. This certainly makes for a more exciting tournament and forces the specialist counter-puncher to adopt a more positive role.

In team competitions, a team generally consists of five karateka plus two reserves or substitutes, and the team with the greatest number of points at the end is declared the winner.

Differences between the styles

As suggested earlier, some style differences are based on

contrasting philosophical and technical attitudes. Some styles see themselves primarily as utilitarian forms of combat, whereas others lay a greater emphasis upon the philosophical undertones of Zen. For some, Zen is irrelevent, whereas for others it is a philosophical support for what is nevertheless primarily a physical activity. Zen, never having been popular in Okinawa, tends to be of minor importance in styles originating there. For a small number of people karate is merely the physical manifestation of the more significant Zen philosophy. In other words the physical and philosophical emphases are reversible.

Apart from this, there are basic physical differences between the styles. Some styles are hard and aggressive, with even the blocks being of a hard, hammer-like nature. Others are gentler and more deflecting in their blocks and more whip- than hammer-like in their attacks. All styles, however, contain an element of both aspects and it is the degree of mix that is variable.

A comparison of these hard and soft elements is best seen within the Goju style. Goju (meaning hard/soft) is based on the Chinese concept of yin and yang, by which everything is understood to consist of combinations of opposites and where an excess of one or the other element is damaging to the organism that contains it. Combinations such as hard/soft, relaxation/tension, fast/slow, male/female, good/bad, etc., are excellent examples. Excessive relaxation can result in lethargy and excessive tension in neurosis. The ideal is a balance between the two. The greatest muscular relaxation is in fact only possible after muscular tension, which is unconsciously why people and cats stretch themselves. Similarly, great tension can only be achieved from a state of relaxation, when the muscles can explode into action. The person who is permanently semi-tense can never achieve either full relaxation or full tension.

Goju utilizes this principle and when attacked with a hard blow the karateka counters with a soft block or deflection and vice-versa. If he countered hard with hard, he would risk injury. By the quick application of tension a soft movement can also quickly become hard and vice-versa. The Goju ideal therefore contains both hard and soft elements, and its Sanchin Kata specifically aims at developing an understanding of the relaxation/tension relationship as well as that between movement and breathing.

As several kata have common origins and have merely been adapted by specific styles for their own particular purpose, there are naturally many common factors as well as differences between the styles. However, in view of the differences in stance, movement, breathing, and emphasis upon speed or power, training katas do quite obviously vary from style to style. Some styles also use kata for different purposes. All consider them to be useful for 'grooving' or memorizing the basic techniques, but not all would agree about their relevance in terms of actual combat. Some believe them to have considerable value in this respect, others very little.

Wood or stone breaking is yet another point on which the emphasis differs. Kyokushinkai place a lot of stress upon it and incorporate it within their grading syllabuses. Most other styles do relatively little breaking or confine it to public demonstrations. The

Gedan-barai (Downward Block). This is a hard 'focused' block to kicks or punches to the lower body. Contact is with the bony inner surface of the arm near the wrist.

extent to which hand calluses are developed again differs and partly reflects the degree to which breaking is practised.

These differences of philosophy and technique help to explain the many styles that exist. When one adds to this today's financial inducements to create new styles and organizations, it is not surprising that the administrative pattern can be confusing to the experienced karateka as well as to the layman.

Modern problems facing karate

Traditionally, in the East, karate was taught on a secretive, small group or family basis. Merely to be accepted into a group involved considerable perseverance until the instructor was convinced of the applicant's, almost even supplicant's, good intentions. Certainly Funakoshi did not teach anyone and everyone. The post-war export of karate from Japan has changed all that. It is now big business without, in the main, the organizational capacity to cope with its changed status.

During the late 1960s and early 1970s, instructors in many different styles poured out of Japan. They created, in opposition to each other, their own tight-knit organizations, each assuming names that were often misleading to the general public in that they suggested full national status without indicating the specialist nature of the style concerned. In the early days they, or their supporters, disputed the credentials of rival styles and sometimes even denied their existence. In Britian alone, in the early 1970s, there were as many as twelve such groups, each claiming national status.

The significance and extent of the differences in style were often in dispute. Sometimes the distinctions were undoubtedly genuine, whereas on other occasions they could quite reasonably be considered nothing more than the result of personality differences or economic motivation. A further problem was that there were often as many groups purporting to represent a country inter-nationally as there were groups in existence. The effect this had upon the standards of international competition is obvious.

With the kung-fu boom of the mid-1970s, some karate instructors, seeing the opportunity for quick profits, restyled themselves as kung-fu experts, and the organizational problems doubled almost overnight. As many countries have no legal restraints to prevent totally unqualified individuals from advertising themselves as karate or kung-fu experts, the social implications can be quite serious. Apart from the risks involved in teaching this type of activity publicly, it is not at all unknown for clubs to open, receive membership fees, and then close down almost immediately.

This chaos is reflected to varying extents in most countries, and each has sought its own solution, many to date without much success. Japan in 1964, at the time of the Tokyo Olympic Games, formed the Federation of All Japan Karate-do Organisations (FAJKO) to try and achieve a degree of co-ordination. France introduced legislation to require all budo instructors, including those for karate, to be licensed by the national association. Britain followed a pattern somewhat similar to Japan and formed a federation of associations in which each group retained its own organizational and stylistic identity. Some other countries have yet to make any attempt to tackle the problem, and the 1970 world championships witnessed the embarrassing spectacle of as many as three quite unrelated teams each claiming to represent one country.

Quite obviously karate is in a period of rapid evolution, which carries with it its own problems. The original close-knit, instructor-based and highly disciplined groups have largely been broken down, due to the pressures of expansion and commercialism. Many clubs are motivated purely by the desire for financial gain, and anyone and everyone is accepted provided the money is handed over. Certainly the concept of a dojo as a 'way place' is becoming increasingly less significant. In some instances clubs are at best merely specialized gymnasiums, whilst at worst, with self-graded instructors, they can be a distinct social danger. It is even possible to purchase correspondence courses in karate. In such circumstances the chances of acquiring the discipline necessary to match fighting skill are almost non-existent.

In this situation, the prime hope for responsible control lies with strong national organizations which embrace all styles and which are capable of maintaining adequate standards and of controlling, and if necessary disciplining, their membership. Whether the national organizational pattern is of a unitary and legislatively supported nature as in France, or of a federal and non-statutory nature as in Britain, is probably a matter of national taste, practical politics, and the apparent extent of the social problem. Such big organizations do of course have their own in-built dangers. The drive for organizational efficiency and financial viability can force into second place or even eliminate the genuine technical and philosophical objectives of karate. However, being aware of this risk, the danger is avoidable. The alternative is anarchy and exploitation.

A soft, deflecting defence with the palm of the hand against a knife attack.

How to find a good club
Generally, when people join a karate club, they do so without very much knowledge of the club they propose to join or the qualifications of the instructor concerned. This is very unwise and often leads to disappointment. First of all you should check what clubs are available in your area. This can normally be done via the national governing body for karate. Make sure that any local clubs are members of this organization and that their instructors are properly qualified. Otherwise grades awarded by them will probably be unrecognized and it will not be possible to enter major competitions. Then decide which style appeals to you and visit the clubs concerned before making your decision. It might well be that one particular instructor's teaching methods are especially suited or unsuited to you. Incidentally, if a club insists on full payment of fees before you are permitted to watch a class in session, have nothing to do with it.

If there is any possibility of your moving to another part of the country, it is also probably worthwhile ensuring that you join a style which has adequate national coverage. To make good progress in one style and then to have to start again in another can be very irritating. It is of course possible to change styles but ideally this should be done through choice rather than necessity.

Related Chinese Arts

Kung fu
Paul Crompton

Tai chi chuan
Paul Crompton

Kung fu

'Kung fu', sometimes referred to as 'gung fu' or 'cong-fou', is a misnomer. 'Kung' means a worker or artist, and 'fu' means a man. The expression therefore means literally a 'man who works with art'. Other translations are simply 'hard work' or 'a man at work'. Another expression connected with Chinese martial arts is 'wu shu', meaning simply 'stop fighting'. That is, the martial art concerned is studied to prevent the occurrence of violence, not to foster it! The idea smacks of the modern notion of a deterrent. Currently both in East and West 'kung fu' is used to mean all the Chinese martial arts. However, this article will largely limit itself to the kung-fu arts which are performed with empty hands.

Theories abound concerning the origins of kung fu, and scholars have noted its appearance over the last 5,000 years. Amongst the most important datings are the following:

1. Kung fu began with the peasant practice of simulated combat wearing a head-dress of horns, which dates from about 2600 BC.

2. It made an appearance in the later Chou dynasty, 1066–403 BC, where there are references to wrestling, archery, fencing, and other tactics.

3. A mild form of kung fu, which took into account the internal side of a man's involvement in life, began during the time of Lao Tzu in the sixth century BC.

4. In the Han dynasty, Hua To, a famous medical man, introduced physical exercises based on animal movements: on the bird, deer, tiger, bear, and monkey.

5. Long before the Mongol invasions of China between 1205 and 1227, boxing was well known and recorded. After the Mongols, many other types of wu shu were developed, principally because of the defeats inflicted upon the Chinese armies of the time. During the subsequent Mongolian invasions of Europe, Chinese/Mongolian styles of wrestling were taken with the invading armies. Lee Ying Yang, a modern kung-fu *sifu*, or teacher, considers that early Chinese/Mongolian combat methods influenced Graeco-Roman empty-hand fighting. Chinese kung fu also spread to Japan, Korea, and many other Far Eastern countries.

6. It is to Bhodidharma or Damo, the bringer of Cha-an meditation or Zen to China in AD 540, that kung-fu students like to attribute the founding of their multi-faceted art. Popular legend has it that Bhodidharma found his monks too weak to maintain his régime of

This bronze plaque from Shansi province, pre-dating the Christian era, is evidence of at least one mode of martial arts: wrestling. The grip being used by the wrestlers has been used ever since, and probably is far more ancient than the plaque itself.

work and meditation and founded a system of leg, arm, and trunk exercises at one of the chain of Shaolin monasteries. This system gave the monks the required strength for their spiritual and physical efforts. Since that time the Shaolin monastries have been foremost in the fostering of kung-fu styles.

Whatever the origins of kung fu, by the eighteenth century missionaries to China were remarking upon it, among them Father Jean Joseph Marie Amiot in his *Short History of China, circa* 1780, who stated:

During the reign of Yn-Kang-Chi the air was always rainy and unhealthy, illness covered the earth like a flood. The Emperor obliged his subjects to do military exercises each day . . . curing those who were unhealthy and maintaining the health of those who were in good condition.

Styles of kung fu

There is hardly an animal, mythical, extinct or extant, which does not have a kung-fu style supposedly based on its distinctive movements. In addition to animal styles, there are styles related to Chinese philosophical ideas. The trigrams of the famous *I-Ching, Book of Changes* are connected by some theorists to the Pa-Kua style of Chinese boxing, with its emphasis on turning in a circle and warding off an opponent by using the palms of the hands. Other styles, for example Tai Chi Chuan and simple single groups of exercises, are said to encourage health and longevity. In variety and multiplicity the styles of kung fu appear to be unique. We can examine only a few here.

In the year AD 629, Hsuan Tsang, a Buddhist monk, was travelling from China to India. Sun Wu-k'ung was his bodyguard, a monkey no less. This legendary monkey employed many means to defend his master and to indulge his own thirst for danger. From his methods, so folklore says, the kung-fu system of Ta Sheng Men or Monkey style developed. The stances of a monkey are adopted in the style, which also employs rolls, crouching defensive positions, and attacking leaps. Like most kung-fu styles, the Monkey style has its sets or what in other martial arts would be termed *katas*. These are linked series of movements devised to teach a student sequences of the style in question.

Tiger style or Hung Gar is, as its name suggests, remarkable for its

152

Ta Sheng Men or Monkey style. Agility and a strong element of surprise are keynotes of this style. Here (*left to right*) the attacker leaps on to his opponent by grabbing his arm or clothing and stepping on his thigh or hip bone. Still pulling on his opponent, the attacker raises his arm to strike, and, when firmly 'on top' of his opponent, he completes his downward chop. This whole sequence is over very quickly, but variations can be devised with a little imagination.

opposite below   An example of the Crane style in which the fully extended arm is swung, like a wing, to deflect a punch. In this case the man on the left swings upward but the method is equally effective at groin level. The powerful 'wings' of Crane stylists can also be used to punch.

below   Another Crane style technique. Here a woman can effectively discourage a man by 'pecking' at a vital spot, such as the eyes.

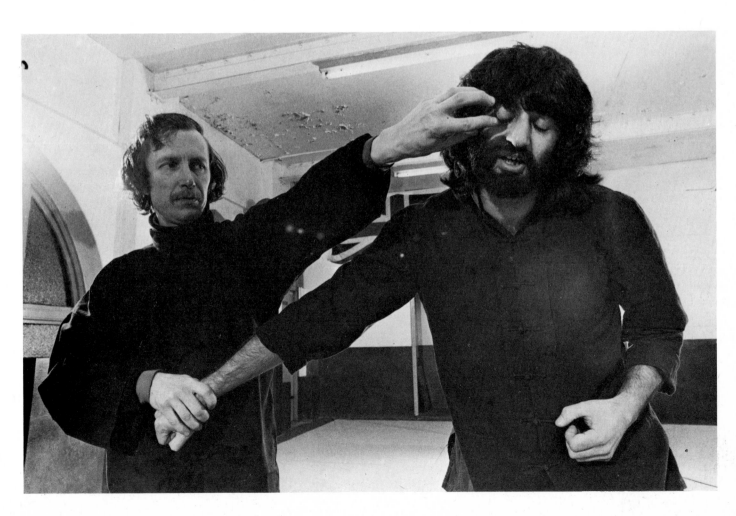

Hung Gar or Tiger style, showing the versatility of its wide stance and the flexibility needed at the waist to take advantage of the stance and punch at an opponent attacking from the right-back corner.

opposite left centre and below Wing Chun. Two typical, swift and economical, simultaneous block-and-punch actions. (*Centre*) The defender thrusts his open, right palm forward and slightly up and out—just enough to deflect the attacker's left-hand punch. At the same time he gives a straight, left 'arrow' punch to the jaw. (*Below*) The defender blocks with the palm of his hand, deflecting the attack to the side or over his shoulder, whilst his left hand delivers a punch.

emphasis on strength, firm stance, long, powerful attacks, and the tiger-claw formation of the hand.

Crane style is based on the powerful beating movements of the crane's wings, which could fracture the arms of an attacker, and also on the sharp, eye-pecking attacks of the crane's beak.

Coming down the scale to the realm of insects, the praying mantis has also made its contribution to kung fu. Founded in the seventeenth century by Master Wong Long, the Praying Mantis style uses fierce grasping movements, clawing attacks, and punches. There is, however, great variety within the style, using as it does the firmness of stance found in Tiger style, a number of movements from the Monkey style, and something of the litheness and antennae-like actions of its namesake.

Within each style of kung fu there are individual methods of standing, placing the feet, and using the arms, knees, head, torso, elbows, wrists, and fingers. But there is hardly a style which has not somewhere within its armoury a 'borrowing' from another style. This is true even of the relatively modern and much publicized Wing Chun style, the favourite of the now legendary Bruce Lee before he evolved his own *tao* of Jeet Kune Do (the Philosophical Way of the Intercepting Fist). Wing Chun was devised by a nun, so the story goes, to help her charges to defend themselves. Economy of movement and directness in defence and attack are the hallmarks of this style. Powerful arms and body are not necessary for it to be effective. Hence its suitability for women. The basic training stance of Wing Chun is not unique; only the concept of economy and directness is peculiar to it alone.

No article on kung fu, however brief, is complete today without reference to Bruce Lee. Leaving aside his film image and the plethora of publicity accompanying it, what of the man? In terms of kung fu he was a man of his era. Just as political, religious, moral, and economic views have been questioned, analysed, refuted, and turned upside-down in modern times, so Lee performed this service(?) for kung fu. He studied many traditional styles before primarily adopting Wing Chun, which is considered something of an 'outlaw' in certain circles. Wing Chun seems, with its casting aside of all encumbrances in the quest for efficiency and economy, to have foreshadowed Lee's personal requirement for a martial art without form, without sets, and without tradition. What he sought was a form which existed only in the individual's ability to respond immediately and instinctively in his own, most appropriate way to a martial-art situation.

Lee has, however, been both misunderstood and misquoted, or rather quoted out of context. He did not mean that no study of traditional forms was required. If that were so, a student of martial arts would have no technique to discard! He surely meant that the basis of his Jeet Kune Do was first an all-round familiarity with the techniques available and then an individual process of selection and discarding, synthesis and analysis, related to the psycho-physical make-up of the man in question. In other words, 'do your own thing' in the martial arts, but first find out what there is to do! Bruce Lee's greatest contribution to the kung-fu world has therefore been the commandment, 'Search!'

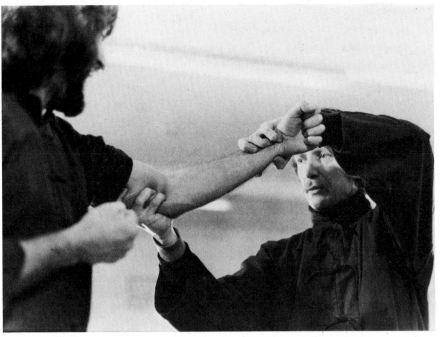

top left   Praying Mantis style. The important points to notice here are the pincer-like grip just above the elbow and the claw-like hold on the wrist. Both inflict pain but they are also a method of securing a firm grip before a sharp pull, throw, or punch.

top   In this Praying Mantis defence technique the defender (*right*) steps to the side to avoid a direct forward attack, at the same time blocking with his left palm and striking at the ribs with his right fist. He is also poised with most weight on his left foot so that the right foot can kick.

above   Mantis students cultivate the independent gripping-power of the fingers. Here the attacker's left wrist has been seized and the pincer-like formation of the defender's right hand strikes various parts of the face.

The secrets of kung fu

In training, kung fu has many different aspects, ranging through muscle-building, with and without apparatus, hand and foot toughening, breaking wood and bricks, breathing exercises, learning the vital points of the body, studying bone-setting and herbal remedies, curing bruising and internal injuries, and using literally almost every part of the body for attack or defence.

The attitudes of different sifu are enormously varied. In bygone centuries secrecy was the watchword. Each style had its secrets and these were jealously guarded. Some styles have been lost forever simply because the last teacher of the style for some reason or other failed to teach another disciple. At some periods challenges to members of other styles were frequent, and regular tournaments have been held since the time of Genghis Khan. Because of the rule of secrecy, potential students often found it difficult to gain admittance to a school of kung fu. A nineteenth-century teacher of Pak Mei was known to like eggs cooked in a particular manner. As a cunning way in, one of his potential students 'accidentally' had a basket of this delicacy with him when he went to plead his case for admission to the Pak Mei circle. Other students were admitted by the more conventional method of patience and obedience until the sifu was finally satisfied about their sincerity.

Today, some of these secrets are still intact. Others have been taught and found to be not so startling as one might have thought. Of the secrets that undoubtedly exist, a fair guess is that they are all related to traditional Chinese knowledge of physiology, breathing, and mental control. Among these are the knowledge of how to retract the testicles, how to withstand severe blows, how to deliver the legendary 'death touch' whose effect is not felt until some time after the blow is struck, and certain skills related to postulated disciplines learned within the confines of the Shaolin temples of old.

It is true to say that many of the so-called secrets of kung fu are only secrets to the quick-result orientated minds of many modern people, both Eastern and Western. Some techniques, some knowledge, come only with time. Kung fu has had over four thousand years. . . .

In this Wing Chun technique the punch is deflected by the defender's leading right arm, his elbow being slightly raised, while the left hand either guides the punching arm away or grabs it, leaving the right hand then free to chop or punch. The whole movement is carried out at very high speed.

Kung fu today

Finally, one should say something about the present state of kung fu. Today it is exploding all over the globe, accompanied by its entourage of experts, fakes, and dedicated students. Authorities in every country are concerned about the violence potential in this boom. There are, of course, many ways of looking at the problem. Kung fu can certainly provide an outlet for energetic, bored youth. At worst it can lead to an interest in violence for its own sake, without any sense of responsibility. At best it can help in the cultivation and growth of an individual. Whichever view you take, there is no denying that for us in the West, kung fu is here to stay.

This sequence from the film *Fist of Fury* demonstrates Bruce Lee's acrobatic skill, as well as his ability in kung fu. It also indicates the star's recognition that kung-fu cinema has to be good 'box office', that is, spectacular. Economy of movement, a feature of his own Jeet Kune Do style, would not have made such a telling impression.

Tai chi chuan

'Tai chi chuan' is translated as 'supreme ultimate fist'. However, any notion that the art resembles karate or kung-fu combat methods should be discarded. Tai chi, as it is known for short, is for most students of the art a system of slow-moving exercise, carried out for health, relaxation, and mental poise. Only a few people understand and are able to use tai chi for combat.

Opinions vary on the origin and date of tai chi. N. Dally, in his book *Cinésiologie au Science du Mouvement*, 1897, refers to Chinese medical gymnastics as far back as 2700 BC. In *Tai Chi for Health*, 1963, Edward Maisel mentions Taoist breathing exercises in existence around 122 BC. The same author speaks of animal-based movements being practised between 25 BC and AD 263. Other writers mention religious dances used to evoke spirits, celebrate an eclipse, meet calamities, accompany civil ceremonies, and so forth. There are no records to make it clear how these dances were performed and so unfortunately attempts to relate them to tai-chi movements are bound to be unsatisfactory. R. W. Smith, co-author of *Asian Fighting Arts*, 1969, provides us with the following theories:
1. The earliest name associated with tai chi is that of Chang San-Feng, a Taoist priest living sometime between AD 1279 and 1368, i.e. the Yuan dynasty. Chang is said to have learned the movements in a dream. However, as even the emissaries of the ruling emperor of the day were unable to find him, this must remain supposition.
2. Tai chi began in the following dynasty (the Ming), under the auspices of the Ch'en family, in Hu-nan.
3. Tai chi dates from sometime during the T'ang dynasty and develops through four schools: Hsu, Yu, Ch'eng, and Yin.
4. Lastly, the theory which Smith himself, an acknowledged authority, finds 'most reasonable'. Tai chi is attributed to one Wang Tsung-yueh during the Ch'ing dynasty: AD 1736–95.

Whatever the truth of it, during the nineteenth century tai chi split up into various schools, and since 1900 individual teachers have modified the methods to such an extent that some of what is now taught as tai chi is barely recognizable as such.

Principles

In considering the principles upon which tai chi is based, we must bear in mind two of the ideas about man and the universe which are part of the Chinese way of life.

A fundamental theme which runs through the whole of Chinese kung fu is the notion that life is maintained by a balance or harmony between two opposite forces: yin and yang. Destruction or imbalance occurs when one force is predominant. This principle applies to man, animals, plants, and the whole of natural life. For example, a plant can exist where there is the right amount of heat and cold. Too much heat or too much cold and it dies. In a man too much relaxation can bring apathy, and too much tension can bring any of our modern stress diseases.

The other important idea is related to Chinese medicine. This is the notion that, in addition to the nervous and circulatory systems known to Western medicine, there exists another palpable system of 'meridians' which carry vital energy to different organs and parts of the body. When this energy is blocked, or when it is running too freely to a particular part or parts, illness ensues.

Now returning to tai chi, it is claimed that through the subtle knowledge which underlies tai-chi movement the forces of yin and yang are harmonized not only in the nervous and circulatory systems but in the finer system of meridians. Breathing, which is fundamental to the proper functioning of all three systems, is also said to benefit and to be brought into harmony by the diligent practice of the art. Other claims are made on its behalf but they can really only be appreciated through practical study.

In a very direct way then, tai chi seems to fulfil the old Western medical belief that the best source of cure or harmony is the *vis medicatrix naturae,* the natural healing power of the body. Man's own tumultuous thoughts and undisciplined emotions cannot help him, but if he can find a way to let his body move and breathe naturally, holding thoughts and emotions in abeyance, then, tai chi says, he can benefit.

A simple body movement during the Beginning Posture of the Long Form.

Methods

Left to himself, man can fluctuate between his most physically quiet state, deep sleep, and the most violent and prolonged exertion imaginable. Tai chi aims at bringing these two extremes closer together. Its object is the maintaining of muscular and nervous relaxation while the body is in movement. Such an effort involves the participation of a watchful mind, and for this reason tai chi has been referred to as 'meditation in movement'.

In trying to 'harmonize with Nature', a student studies the effect of gravity on the body. Gravity pulls everything down. So tai chi teaches a particular way of placing the feet so that, like a tree, the body can be well rooted. The spine, on which the vital organs of the body depend, is coaxed into an optimum, vertical position. The shoulders are allowed to respond to gravity, and are lowered. The head is balanced on the top of the spine and not allowed to loll or be pulled forward by tension of the neck muscles. When a hand is lifted the elbow is kept low, once more following the path of least resistance to the pull of gravity. And all the time correct muscle tone is encouraged.

As his study of tai chi deepens, the student finds that the tension, almost inevitably associated with learning new, apparently complex movements, falls away. He recognizes that he is using a great deal

The Single Whip, one of the more complex movements of tai chi. (*Left to right*) Turning away from a preceding move known as Push, the performer takes both arms round horizontally, turning the feet inwards. The left foot swivels on to the ball of the toes whilst the left hand cups a swan-like formation of the right hand, the body by this time having moved through almost 180 degrees. The right hand moves back away from the body, and the left palm, facing the eyes and watched throughout the movement, travels in a forward-moving arc. The left foot steps out, and the body-weight shifts mostly on to the left foot as the left hand turns palm away from the body, the eyes looking over the fingers of the hand.

below Tai chi with a partner. Each has the wrist lightly resting on the partner's wrist. The partner on the left 'pushes' forward, using all her body-weight but only 'attached' at the wrist. The one on the right yields, turning in a circle at the waist. In his turn the right-hand partner 'pushes' at the wrist and the left-hand partner yields. The partner on the right continues to push and so the girl is able to pull him off balance.

Two tai chi kicking techniques: (*left*) Separate Right Foot and (*right*) Strike with Sole. In the former the right leg swings freely upwards from the hip without strain, and in the latter the knee is bent up towards the chest and the leg then extended, toes pointing up.

more muscular effort than is necessary. As he begins to relax more, the vital energy, the nervous system, the blood circulation, and the breathing become easier. With assiduous study the increased relaxation achieved can be carried over into everyday life, thereby creating a counter to the increased physical and psychological pressures of modern living.

Compared with many other methods of Chinese boxing, tai chi is, for the most part, a long demanding study. This is because tai chi is an 'internal' method. Mere parrot learning of a series of physical movements plays no part in it. Smashing bricks and wood, leaping sixteen feet in the air, crippling opponents with rib-crushing blows, all find no place in tai chi. Such displays are for the external styles, the ones that have no time for harmony.

Movements
The core of tai-chi movements is the Long Form. This consists of 108 linked movements which nowadays are generally learned as a series of completed postures and subsequently joined together into a continuous flowing action. It is a hard lesson, but one proven through experience, that most Western people learn these 108 postures best if they learn them slowly. That is to say, if they learn no more than one or two postures per session. Tai chi really bears out the old adage: 'Make haste slowly.' In tai chi you can get away with nothing. Every part of the body must be in the correct position. The principles of movement remain the same, but people find it hard to remember principles and have to be re-taught at every turn.

Some of the movements of tai chi are very simple in basic execution. The Beginning Posture, for example, is deceptively so, whereas the Single Whip is undeniably complex. Yet both, when known, can be carried out with virtually the same amount of effort.

Later in the Long Form various kicking movements appear. They are, however, not called 'kicking' but rejoice in the titles of 'separate right foot' and 'separate left foot', indicating that no feeling of aggression or force is involved—merely that one leg is 'separating' from another.

There are some postures which are very difficult to execute in the correct fashion, notably Single Whip Squatting Down, which can do more harm than good if carried out incorrectly. But here again, it will only be done incorrectly if force is used and the student departs from the principles of tai chi.

In learning to link the various postures of tai chi together, the student discovers that he is constantly and rhythmically shifting the weight of his body from one leg to the other, alternately tensing and relaxing his leg muscles, raising and lowering his arms, rotating his body from side to side, expanding and sinking his chest, and so on. He becomes in fact a dynamic expression of the fundamental idea of yin and yang harmony. However, this does not come in a day. . . . The movements are learned gradually and alone until a student can turn his efforts towards studying with a partner.

With a partner

Having appreciated the spirit of tai chi within himself, what about the world outside? If someone pushes me, if a force in effect is applied to me, how can I deal with it?

Most people, if pushed, resist. They oppose force with force. In terms of yin and yang both people are applying the same type of force at the same point. Admittedly, the stronger will overcome, but both men will have used a great deal of energy in the struggle. Supposing one of the partners or antagonists were to give way, to yield, then the force of the aggressor would carry him forward. In theory at least, with a little more force added by the man who was yielding, the aggressor could be overbalanced, even thrown over.

Tai chi approaches this idea subtly. Two students face each other, the backs of one wrist and lower forearm lightly resting together. One student pushes forward with his whole body, his contact arm being merely an extension of the entire mass of his body, whilst the other student yields, turning at the waist and 'leading' his partner round and forward at the same time. Contact is maintained all the while, and, as the limit of the forward circular movement is reached, it is the turn of the 'defender' to push forward and the turn of the 'attacker' to yield. Variations on this method are learned, but the principle is always the same: if the attacker pushes too hard, then by yielding the defender can lure him forward and cause him to lose his balance. Hence the student learns about his weight, his balance, and his psychological reactions to another person. Through learning to apply the principles of the Solo Exercise of the Long Form, he is able to play a harmonious duet!

Today, through the rapid proliferation of books and magazines, tai chi chuan is becoming widespread. All kinds of muddled ideas are congregating around it. Basically, however, it is a real and useful gift from the Orient, but a gift which has to be studied in a practical way for its benefits to be experienced.

Table of chronology

Summary of Japanese historical periods

Archaic Period pre 552 AD

BC 660	Legendary founding of Japanese empire by Jimmu Tenno. Origins of Shinto, Japan's most widespread religion.
early 4th century BC	Japan partly unified.

Asuka Period 552–645 AD

Buddhism introduced from China.
Subsequent strong influence on Japanese arts.

Nara Period 645–794 AD

646 AD	Japan adopts centralized bureaucratic system of Chinese empire.
710 AD	Nara, Japan's first permanent capital, laid out on lines of Chinese capital.
741 AD	Buddhism becomes state religion. Japanese culture strongly influenced by mainland China.

Heian Period 794–1185 AD

1185 AD	Ending of the epic struggle of Taira and Minamoto clans in the latter's victory.

Kamakura Period 1185–1333 AD

1192 AD	Minamoto Yoritomo becomes first shogun, setting up military headquarters at Kamakura. Emergence of *bushido*, a written code of warrior ethics. Zen Buddhism develops.

Ashikaga or Muromachi Period 1333–1568 AD

1333 AD	Emperor Go-Daigo destroys Kamakura. Fifty-year struggle for succession, basically a struggle for redistribution of feudal power.

1477 AD	Collapse of central government following the Onin War (1467–77).
1500 AD	All Japan at war. Many peasant uprisings. Matchlocks introduced into battle.

Azuchi-Momayamo Period 1568–1615 AD

1568 AD	Nobunaga becomes *de facto* shogun, destroys warring monasteries, and crushes Buddhism as political force.
1582 AD	Hideyoshi succeeds Nobunaga, unifies country, and imposes peace.
1598 AD	Ieyasu succeeds Hideyoshi, becomes first official Tokugawa shogun, and sets up Edo as administrative capital. By defeating rebel chieftains, gains control of Japan.
1612 AD	End of Sengoku-Jidai era or Age of the Country at War.

Edo or Tokugawa Period 1615–1868 AD

1783–7 AD	Rice riots. Growing opposition to shogunate.
1838 AD	Famines. Shogunate financially embarrassed.
1868 AD	Shogunate overthrown and power restored to emperor. Imperial court moves to Edo (renamed Tokyo) to join administrative court.

Meiji Period 1868–1912 AD

	Under Emperor Meiji, Japan begins programme of modernization, westernization, and territorial expansion.
1871 AD	Disestablishment of samurai.
1874 AD	Punitive expedition against Formosa to ease samurai dissatisfaction.
1876 AD	Samurai forbidden to wear two swords. Establishment of conscript army of all classes. Samurai dissatisfaction culminates in Satsuma rebellion.

Bibliography

Below is a list of books, each of which was recommended by at least one of the contributors. Some of them are no longer in print but they should all be available from public libraries.

General

Asian Fighting Arts by Donn F. Draeger and Robert W. Smith. Kodansha, Tokyo, 1969. Ward Lock, London, 1969.

Classical Budo by Donn F. Draeger. Weatherhill, New York, 1973.

Classical Bujutsu by Donn F. Draeger. Weatherhill, New York, 1973.

A First Zen Reader edited by Trevor P. Leggett. Tuttle, Tokyo, and Rutland, Vermont, 1960.

A History of Japan (3 vols.) by Sir George Sansom. Stanford University Press, California, 1958–63. Barrie & Jenkins, London, 1959–64.

Modern Budo and Bujutsu by Donn F. Draeger. Weatherhill, New York, 1974.

The Three Pillars of Zen edited by Philip Kapleau. Harper & Row, New York, 1966, and London, 1967.

Weaponry

Japanese Archery: Zen in Action by André Sollier and Zsolt Gyorbiro. Weatherhill, New York, 1969.

Zen in the Art of Archery by Eugen Herrigel (translated by R. F. C. Hull). Routledge, London, 1953. Pantheon, New York, 1953.

Unarmed Combat

Aikido by Morei Uyeshiba. Wehman, Hackensack, New Jersey, 1968.

Aikido and the Dynamic Sphere by Adele Westbrook and Oscar Ratti. Tuttle, Tokyo, and Rutland, Vermont, 1970.

Aikido in Daily Life by Koichi Tohei. Japan Publications, Tokyo, 1973.

The Book of Sumo: Sport of Wrestling by Doug Kenrick. Weatherhill, New York, 1969, and London, 1972.

Championship Judo by Trevor P. Leggett and K. Watanabe. Foulsham, Slough, 1964.

Contest Judo by Saburo Matsushita and Warwick Stepto. Foulsham, Slough, 1961. Sterling, New York, 1962.

Dynamic Karate by Masatoshi Nakayama. Kodansha, Tokyo, 1967. Ward Lock, London, 1967.

Fundamentals of Goju-ryu Karate by Gosei Yamaguchi. Wehman, Hackensack, New Jersey, 1973.

Illustrated Kodokan Judo. Japanese Publications, Tokyo, 1955.

Judo: How to Become a Champion by John Goodbody. Luscombe, London, 1974.

Karate-do by Tatsuo Suzuki. Pelham, London, 1975 (second edition).

Know Karate-do by Bryn Williams. Luscombe, London, 1975.

Know the Game: Judo by the British Judo Association. Educational Productions, London (published yearly).

Modern Karate by Steve Arneil and Bryan Dowler. Kaye and Ward, London, 1974.

The Principles and Practice of Aikido by Senta Yamada and Alex Mackintosh. Foulsham, Slough, 1966. Wehman, Hackensack, New Jersey, 1966.

Sumo: The Sport and the Tradition by J. A. Sargeant. Tuttle, Tokyo, and Rutland, Vermont, 1959.

Related Chinese Arts

Secrets of Shaolin Temple Boxing edited by Robert W. Smith. Tuttle, Tokyo, and Rutland, Vermont, 1964.

T'ai-chi: The Supreme Ultimate Exercise for Health, Sport and Self-Defense by Cheng Man-ch'ing and Robert W. Smith. Tuttle, Tokyo, and Rutland, Vermont, 1967.

Acknowledgments

People and Organizations
The publishers gratefully acknowledge the help and
encouragement of all those who attended the photographic
sessions and thank the following clubs and organizations who
made their premises available for photographic purposes: the
Brighton Boys' Club, Edward Street, Brighton; the Budokwai,
Gilston Road, London; the London Judo Society, St Oswald's
Place, London; and the National Sports Centre, Crystal Palace,
London.

Photographs
Unless otherwise indicated all the action photographs in this
book were taken on behalf of the publishers by Bob Hope, and
the Japanese prints were photographed at the Victoria and
Albert Museum by Graham Portlock.

All-Japan Kendo Renmei, Tokyo 33 (*bottom*)
All-Japan Kyudo Renmei, Tokyo 40–1, 41 (*bottom left*), 42
All-Japan Naginata-do Renmei, Osaka 50
Associated Press, London 14, 86, 138 (*top*)
Basketball Magazine, Tokyo 69 (*bottom*), 70, 71, 72, 73, 74, 75
British Kendo Renmei 23 (*top*)
Ken Broome contents page, 127 (*left*), 127 (*right*)
Camera Press, London 10 (*bottom right*)
Cathay Films 157 (*top*), 157 (*bottom*)
Contemporary Films 20 (*bottom*)
Jim Elkin 109
David Finch 101 (*bottom*), 102, 103, 104
Hamlyn Group Picture Library (Réalités) 10 (*top*)
Bob Hope 15, 132 (*top*)
Keystone Press Agency, London 32, 85, 101 (*top*)
Roald Knutsen 7 (*top left*), 20 (*centre*), 21, 23 (*bottom*),
    29 (*top right*), 33 (*top*), 37, 54 (*bottom*), 55 (*top*),
    55 (*bottom*)
Mainichi Shinbun, Tokyo 35, 36 (*bottom left*)
Mirror Newspapers, London 13 (*top*)
Popperfoto, London 51

Publishers
Grateful acknowledgment is given to the following publishers:
Charles E. Tuttle Company, Inc., Tokyo and Rutland, and their
book *The Hokusai Sketch-books: Selections from the 'Manga'*
by James A. Michener (1958), for the illustrations on pages
40 (*top*), 54 (*top*), and 79 (*right*); Kodansha International,
Tokyo, and their book *Asian Fighting Arts* by Donn F. Draeger
and Robert W. Smith (1969), for the illustrations on pages 77
and 151; Routledge and Kegan Paul, London, and their book
Tales of Old Japan by A. B. Mitford/Lord Redesdale (1966),
for the illustration on page 78; and Rikugei Publishing, Tokyo,
and their book *Aikido: The Arts of Self-Defense* by Koichi
Tohei (1961), for the illustration on page 108.

Index

Figures in italics refer to illustrations

Wausa Public Schools
Wausa, Nebraska 68786